EMOTIONAL
ROOTS
OF SINUSITIS
And Tools to Heal Them

EMOTIONAL

ROOTS

OF SINUSITIS

And Tools to Heal Them

Alice Briggs

Emotional Roots of Sinusitis
And Tools to Heal Them

ISBN: 978-1-948666-40-4

Published by:
Alice Arlene, Ltd. Co.
Lubbock, TX, 79493

For those who do not give up the fight in their pursuit of healing

Then the Lord God formed the man of dust from the ground, and breathed into his nostrils the breath of life; and the man became a living person.
Genesis 2:7 NASB

Contents

Introduction

OVER THE LAST twenty or more years, I've become more and more interested in the hidden reasons for sicknesses of all sorts. My master's degree is in occupational therapy, and I love the medical community and scientific research. But as I was working with patients, I noticed that medicine didn't have an explanation for much that was happening. As I learned about spiritual warfare and emotional blockages, these key components were obviously missing in a medical treatment plan.

I realized that for the most part, allopathic medicine had significant limitations in helping people to live a life free of dis-ease—a life of wellness and wholeness. But as I connected with others with this belief, I found that many of them rejected the medical community because of their focus on treating what had gone wrong rather than a pursuit of wellness.

So often, humans swing from one extreme to another. Doctors and those in the medical community are either almost worshipped, or they're despised. I think a more moderate approach is closer to the truth and a better way to look at these matters. Medicine isn't all there is that's helpful, but it is the best place to go for many issues. If you fall and break your arm, you need someone who's skilled to set it. If you are dealing with a chemical imbalance in your system, you may need the help of medication to balance you. If you've been in an accident, you may need the skills and abilities of the emergency personnel on the scene and at the hospital.

It is fair to say that medicine is focused on an absence of illness, which is not the same thing as true health and well-being. For that, you may need better nutrition, supplements, and exercises. In addition, you will need the help of various professionals trained to assess your needs and goals who can help you make the right choices to achieve those goals.

But no amount of nutrition and supplementation will set your arm. It may work too slowly to heal a chemical imbalance. And it probably won't do you a lot of good at the scene of an accident. Will they increase your healing and provide better outcomes? Undoubtably. But both are needed.

My opinion is that medical treatment and alternate treatments both have value. They are both—or maybe it would be better to say all—tools to help you survive and live a better life. But just as with any tool, you need to know what tool to use and when to use it for the most optimal success. A screwdriver will not help you put a nail in the wall to hang a picture, and a hammer will not screw the cover on the light switch. That doesn't mean the screwdriver is good and the hammer is bad or vice versa; it just means that they were created for a purpose, and you'll get the best results if you use the right tool for the right job.

So it is in the realm of our health. Consider your options and make the decision that best fits your situation. If you find something better later, then switch to that. But don't feel any condemnation for making the best choice you could at the time.

Spiritual and Emotional Health

As people are becoming more and more interested in overall health and being vibrantly alive instead of just not ill, they recognize that they might not just need healing in the physical realm. We are triune beings. We have a body, soul, and a spirit. And you can't separate them. Each one affects the others. Physical issues will take their toll on the spirit and soul in much the same way that issues in the soul can take their toll on the physical and spiritual, and spiritual issues will affect the soul and body.

In our search to understand any of the three areas of our beings, we often have ignored the other two. It's fine to start with that premise; it's easier to study something and see how it works in isolation than as part of a complex whole. The problem is that we don't bring that understanding back into the greater whole and seek to understand how it affects the rest of our being.

The difficulty, of course, is that we are all created uniquely and are very complex creatures. So we struggle to find a definitive answer. When you're dealing with a bacterial infection, the physical processes involved are well understood in the physical realm, but not necessarily so in the emotional or spiritual realms.

In the discussion of the physical and emotional roots of viruses that follow, understand that I am giving you a set of tools that may help you. Emotional and physical roots of any disease have some similarities between people, but there is still a lot we don't know. I've gathered various resources that discuss these roots, and there is some consensus among them, but they don't all say the same thing. I'm going to share what I've found with you, and I'm going to give you tools to address the root causes and point you toward other resources you might find helpful. This is a toolkit: See what tools you think will benefit you the most and start there.

EMOTIONAL ROOTS OF SINUSITIS

And Tools to Heal Them

Emotional Roots of Sinusitis

Sinusitis

SINUSITIS IS THE inflammation of the spaces inside your head, called the sinuses. It can be an acute condition, often caused by the common cold,[1] or chronic when symptoms persist for three months or longer despite treatment.[2] If you've had either, you're all too familiar with the stuffy nose, congestion, tenderness, and pressure. You might also experience ear pressure, headache, aching in your teeth, altered smell, cough, bad breath, fatigue, and fever. Quite a few physical causes might contribute to sinusitis, but you're probably aware of all those if this is an issue for you, and I'll leave those discussions to you and your doctor or other medical professional.

I find it interesting that the nose is symbolic of intuition. Maybe this is because Genesis 2:7 tells us that God breathed life into man through his nostrils. I've heard this saying all my life: something "smells wrong" in the sense that something isn't right. Or people say that it doesn't pass the "sniff test." I wonder, since God gave mankind life through the nose,

---

1   "Acute Sinusitis," Mayo Clinic, accessed April 22, 2022, https://www.mayoclinic.org/diseases-conditions/acute-sinusitis/symptoms-causes/syc-20351671.

2   "Chronic Sinusitis," Mayo Clinic, accessed April 22, 2022, https://www.mayoclinic.org/diseases-conditions/chronic-sinusitis/symptoms-causes/syc-20351661.

if what we're really saying is that whatever smells off is out of alignment with that breath of heaven. Our spiritual sense of smell is our sense of discernment, and we can spot the fake because it isn't the true. And I think that the emotional roots of issues with sinuses support that hypothesis.

The Emotional Roots of Sinusitis

THE EMOTIONAL ROOTS of sinus troubles are fear, anxiety, stress, tension, and insecurity on one side. On the other, there's control, dominating, possessiveness, and being irritated by someone close to you. It makes sense to me that the first list is probably the deepest one, and the second list is how we try to cope with those issues in the first list. So often, human nature wants to control what we can when we feel anxious or fear about something.

Discernment is clearly a gift of God, so I think that part of what happens here is that we have the gift, but we don't know what to do with it. We sense something isn't right, but we don't know what's wrong or how to handle the situation. This creates negative emotions, and if we don't process them and the situation correctly, they can cause all the issues above throughout our entire systems: physically, mentally, emotionally, and spiritually.

For several years, I struggled with chronic sinusitis. In looking back, this was a time of great uncertainty and stress for me on several levels, and I was learning how to give up control. I didn't know then what I know now about spiritual warfare and fighting the good fight of faith, and so those issues manifested in my physical body, depleting my strength and energy. I'll share one of the most powerful tools I learned that has helped me and many others in the tools that follow.

Toolkit

TAKE NOTE OF any of the roots above that resonate with you and work through any or all of the following tools for them as a group or individually. Repeat as needed. Often, especially if this has been a longstanding issue for you, your system has a habit to overcome, so the repetition helps rewire your system toward the positive for ongoing healing and wholeness.

Prayer

This is a very simple prayer. The power isn't in lots of flowery words, but it's in listening and obeying. I've used this prayer in multiple situations. Not always do I get an answer to what's wrong, but I always get an answer to what I'm supposed to do. More often than not, it's just to pray and then I do so as I feel led. Sometimes, there's a prophetic act that I'm to do, which can be as simple as a slight gesture of my hand or arm. I don't always know what the result is for the situation, but the result for me is always profound. I'm able to rest at peace knowing I did what God asked and out of that obedience, whatever I could do, I have done and I can let God and others do the rest.

A tool that's helped here as well is the flower essence Yarrow Shield. I didn't realize how much of what was happening around me I was taking on as mine until I started taking the essence. What it does for me is that I can still sense whatever it is, but I know it's not mine. This way, I don't take it home with me! That may sound silly, but it's been incredibly powerful for me as I work with people or am just out and about in my community.

Father, I sense something is not right here.

What is wrong?

What do you want me to do about it?

Energetic Release

And I do mean real energy, like electricity. Negative emotions can get stuck in our systems, but we can easily release them using circuitry and intention. Circuitry operates much like the electricity in your house, where the light bulb is off until you flip the switch. This completes the circuit, allows the electrical energy to flow, and the light turns on. Intention refers to our intention to release the negativity that is the key to unlocking it. You use your hands and touch certain points, depending on where the emotion or the circuit is stored. With one hand, touch one of the points on the diagrams to follow with your fingertips, and with your other hand, touch a head point with your fingertips. Touch your forehead if this feels as if it's always been an issue, touch the top of your head if you feel it is coming at you from someone else, touch your left temple if it's mainly in the past, or touch your right temple if you feel this about the future. Think about releasing the emotion related to that point. You don't have to feel the emotion or identify its source, just intend to release the emotion. Hold for a few minutes or until you feel the energy release.

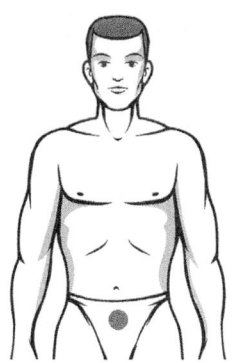

Bladder: fear, irritation

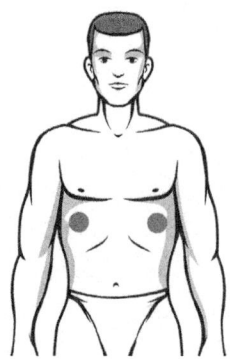

Spleen: Anxiety, insecurity, possessiveness

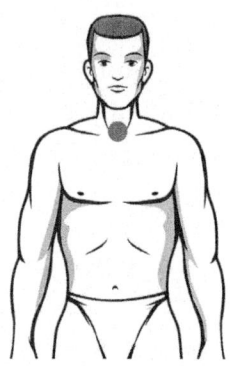

Thyroid: stress, tension

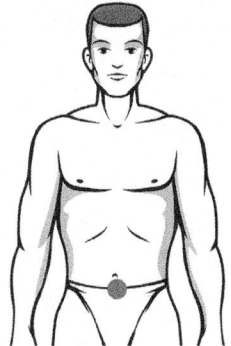

Large Intestine: Control, dominating

Books by Me

I've included each of these later in this book, but I include them here so you can choose the tools that you feel will be best for you to begin with. Each book walks you through emotional and spiritual healing strategies so you won't need to listen to those lies ever again.

Including:

- Generational Issues
- Ungodly Beliefs and Lies
- Emotional Wounds
- Demonic Oppression
- And more!
- Plus strategies to walk out the healing you've received.

Overcoming Anxiety

- **Are you anxious and afraid?**
- **Do you fear the present or the future?**
- **Does worry consume your thoughts?**

If so, you may need some healing from anxiety.

Anxiety tells you that the future is scary, and gives you pictures of all the horrible things that can and will go wrong. It churns all the fear in your stomach until you want to run away and hide. Anxiety says that nothing good will happen to you.

Anxiety lies.

Overcoming Insecurity

- **Do you often feel unloved or unsafe?**
- **Are you overly self-conscious, afraid that people will not accept you?**

If so, you may need some healing from insecurity.

Insecurity tells you that you will not be safe or secure. It tells you that no one will care about you or like or love you because of who you are or something about you. Insecurity tells you that you need to not try because it won't work for you.

Insecurity lies.

Overcoming Control

- **Do you feel that you are being controlled?**
- **Do you feel the need to be in control of everything?**

If so, you may need some healing from control.

Control tells you that you need to be under someone's thumb at all times or you'll run amok. Or, it tells you that you have to control everything around you or you won't be able to be safe, or get anything done. Control tells you that control equals love.

Control lies.

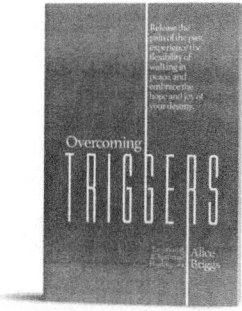

Overcoming Triggers

- **Do some things make you feel like a child again, right back when you were hurt?**
- **Do you get unreasonably angry or upset with some people?**
- **Do some things make you feel like a child again, right back when you were hurt?**

If so, you may need some healing from triggers.

Triggers tell you that your current situation will turn out exactly like the one when you were a child. That you're still as helpless as you were then. Triggers put you right back in your memory of hurts at all ages and tell you that it will always be the same. The people today will hurt you like the people in the past.

Triggers lie.

Overcoming Jealousy

- **Do you have a hard time celebrating when others succeed?**
- **Do you believe that you have to be better than anyone else?**
- **Are you afraid that others will take what you have?**

If so, you may need some healing from jealousy.

Jealousy tells you that if others do better than you in an area that you are worthless. Envy of what others have consumes you because without being on top you're at the bottom. Jealousy tells you that your identity is bound in what others have or do and you have to keep others from stealing from you.

Jealousy lies.

Flower Essences

I highly recommend flower essences and have been using them myself for many years now. I trust the essences from Freedom Flowers because I personally know Seneca, and I know she operates from and with the right spirit in making her essences. I won't go into all the details, as you can find out more about what she offers on her site. If the descriptions of these don't fit you, she offers a custom combo HERE.

Stay Calm Flower Essence may help with:

- Calming the "fight or flight" response
- Giving optimism, gladness, courage, and enthusiasm
- The ability to face difficult situations
- Facilitating deep natural relaxation
- Removing fear so revelation can surface
- Dealing with intimidations, shyness, and public speaking nerves
- The ability to put opinions, thoughts, and ideas out there without fear
- The ability to see the bigger picture
- Prevent panicking
- Stopping ruminations and worries

Good Grief Flower Essence can help with:

- Crying if you need to, or stopping it if you can't quit
- Going the fastest route through the grieving process
- Soothing during a time of emotional distress
- Releasing emotional pain of heartbreak and co-dependency
- Releasing painful emotions
- Assisting with relationships that end
- Lifting up a heavy heart
- Facing difficult situations
- Neutralizing any kind of trauma

Peace Flower Essence may help with:

- Releasing bitterness and resentment
- Getting along with others
- Finding peace during stressful events
- Winding down after work
- Dissolving fear, anger and frustration
- Taking down walls of self-protection
- Soothing central nervous system
- Regaining balance and flexibility in life

Yarrow Shield may help with:

- Being less affected by others' moods
- Feeling less bombarded when out in public
- Setting boundaries for empathetic or Highly Sensitive people
- Effects from multiple chemical sensitivity, EMF's or allergies
- Protection from someone's anger and negativity
- Blocking deliberate "projected" energy from other people
- Sensory overload
- Feeling overwhelmed and overloaded by emotions

Healing Frequencies Music

I also strongly recommend music created by Del Hungerford with the intention to heal and using specific frequencies. Del has researched the frequencies she uses for accuracy and maximum benefit. Click the album to be taken to Del's site to purchase. This is great music to play softly in the background as you go throughout your day.

Books by Others

I've found these particularly helpful in my research for these books, although I don't necessarily agree with everything they believe or have written. As with anything, including anything I've written, I recommend you keep the meat and spit out the bones. Click on each topic for more information or to purchase.

- Living Pain Free by Dr. Devi S. Nambudripad D.C., L.Ac., R.N., Ph.D.
- Resetting Your Emotions by Dr. Devi S. Nambudripad D.C., L.Ac., R.N., Ph.D.
- Feelings Buried Alive Never Die… by Karol K Truman
- A More Excellent Way by Dr. Henry W. Wright
- Heal Your Body by Louise Hay

Emotional and Spiritual Healing Books

Oveercoming Anxiety

Overcoming Insecurity

Overcoming Control

Overcoming Triggers

Overcoming Jealousy

How to Read and
Use these Books

THIS IS A toolbox. Just like plumbing or building, you have an end goal in mind, but you can reach that goal via several paths. The chapters are tools, and you can use them in any order you choose. I've placed them in the order I've found effective for many, but I give you complete freedom to create the order that works best for you. I recommend that you leave the chapter on demonic oppression for last. You will find it easier to complete the other steps first.

Your path to healing is your own. It will not look like anyone else's. That's how it should be. The point is to continue to move forward.

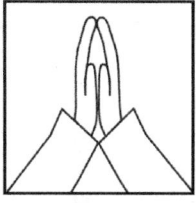

Throughout the books, I have included scripted prayers for your use with this praying hands icon by each one so that you can easily find them. These prayers are suggestions only. Add more to the prayer or deviate from it entirely if you choose. This work is between you and God. Always follow his leading first. If you are familiar with the concepts I discuss, you can skip straight to the prayers.

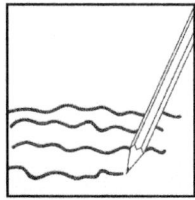

You will also find sections with this journaling icon. These are perfect opportunities to journal or to listen and write what you hear the Lord saying to you about the topic.

Especially in the prayers, I'll refer to the enemy. You are probably familiar with this term, but in case it is new to you, I wanted to include a brief explanation here. The Bible often refers to Satan or the devil as our enemy. In Revelation 12:9, he deceives the entire world. In 1 Peter 5:8, he is seeking people to devour. In John 10:10, he is the thief who comes to steal, kill, and destroy. The devil is not omnipresent as God is, so he is probably not personally attacking you. He has an unknown number (believed to be one-third of the angels per Revelation 12:4) of demons who go about doing his will. Thus, the enemy in this context refers to any demons who are working against God's plans and purposes in our lives.

We don't know their names, and we don't need to. We refer to them according to their function: depression, affliction, poverty, etc. This is their primary activity in our lives. In Christ, we have complete authority over all the works of the enemy because of his death on the cross and his resurrection. In Matthew 28:18-19, after Christ was resurrected, he tells his disciples that all authority in heaven and earth had been given to him, and therefore they could go and make disciples. Because of this, some don't even think that inner healing is necessary.

If we have all authority, then the enemy has none and can't harass us. In my view and in the view of many others, there is a difference between what we can access and what we actively participate in. Often we aren't aware of the enemy or of our authority, and so he operates more freely because of our ignorance than he has the right to do. A thief has no right to take my car or wallet, but he can still do so if I leave them unguarded. The spiritual realm functions in the same manner. Once the car or wallet is in his possession, I must take action to retrieve them.

Sometimes we give the enemy rights he would not otherwise have because we come into agreement with what he says about us. When we hear, "You're stupid," and we think, "Yes, that's right, I'm stupid," we give the enemy the right to keep repeating those lies to us. It's as if we allow the enemy to use our car or wallet to do whatever he wants. We've given him that right. But because Christ gave us all authority, we can take those rights away from the enemy. I've designed the prayers in this book to do that for you.

I've structured the book in the order I typically find the most useful for gaining victory. But again, please use the book in whatever way works best for you and your journey.

Prepare for Healing

HAVE FAITH IN God's promises for healing and restoration. His Word is true. He is who he says he is, and he can do what he says he can do. Faith is choosing to believe and trust not only in who he is, but that his words to you are true. The Bible tells us that faith is the expectation of things hoped for and the belief in things unseen (Hebrews 11:1). Without faith, it is impossible to please God (Hebrews 11:6). And faith comes by hearing, and hearing by the Word of Christ (Romans 10:17).

I recommend, especially if you are disappointed and discouraged by a lack of progress and/or healing in any area, that you begin by searching through the Bible to find those verses that speak to God's ability and willingness to save, heal, and deliver you. Read the stories of healing and deliverance found throughout the Word, but especially in the gospels where Jesus healed and set so many free. God is not a respecter of persons (Acts 10:34); what he has done for one, he can and will do again.

Another great study to increase your faith is to investigate the meaning of the original Greek word translated as "salvation," *sozo*.[3] This word means being saved from your sins, but it also means healing and deliverance. Again, watch how Jesus demonstrated this as he walked on the earth. He didn't just save people but healed and delivered them from many difficulties. This even

---

3 "Strong's G4982 – sōzō," Blue Letter Bible, accessed April 22, 2019, https://www.bluelet-terbible.org/lang/lexicon/lexicon.cfm?t=kjv&strongs=g4982.

included financial freedom as he caused a fish to have a coin in its mouth sufficient to pay the temple tax for him and a disciple. Salvation is a much more comprehensive concept than we typically think of in the church today. But we're learning!

Once you have several verses in hand, personalize them. Write them out as if God wrote them especially for you. Then read them aloud to yourself at least three to five times a day until you feel faith arising within you for your healing.

Set Your Intention for Healing and Freedom

Decide within yourself that you will pursue healing and deliverance until you achieve your goal. Most of the time, healing happens in layers as we gain a measure of freedom step-by-step. God can, and sometimes does, heal and deliver people instantly, but often it is more of a process. I know for myself, I've often not followed through with walking out my healing and have relapsed into old habits. I'll talk more about practical steps to walk out your healing later, but determine in your heart now that you will not only be courageous enough to be healed, but you will also be courageous enough to continue to pursue healing until those old habits shatter.

Realize that God might heal you instantly, but he also might take you through layers of healing as you unlearn bad habits and replace them with good ones. But healing will come either way.

Allow Yourself Time and Grace for the Process

Give yourself time and grace to do the following:
- Think, pray, and prepare before you begin the healing process
- Work through the process in your journey.
- Walk out your healing and freedom.
- Learn better habits and coping strategies.

Celebrate your wins. Focus your attention on the progress you've made, and don't listen to the enemy as he tries to pull you back in the pit you've just climbed out of or another pit beside it. God is counting the number of times you get up and try again. He is counting the steps you take. He isn't counting how many times you trip and fall. For example, the Bible tells us that Abraham made many mistakes and acted less than faithful, but that's not what God remembers. Genesis 15:6 (NLT) states that God counted Abraham as righteous. And God sees you as righteous too.

Remember watching a baby learning to walk. They are horrible at it. They wobble all over the place; they constantly fall down. As walkers or runners, they're not very successful. But when the mom calls grandma, what does she tell her? How many steps baby took. Mom never mentions how many times the baby fell or how wobbly she is. The mom expresses sheer delight in the progress the baby has made. No one expects the baby to run a marathon!

That's how God sees us; I'm convinced of it. He understands perfectly where we've been and what we've been through. God doesn't expect us to instantly do something perfectly that we've never done before. He delights in every step we take. We're the ones—not God—who seem to think we should go from the cradle to the gold-medal platform at the Olympics.

Give yourself the same grace he gives you for your journey. God is with you. He is leading you and putting resources in front of you so that you can find your way home or find your way to increased healing.

Don't Listen to the Can'ts

Don't listen to the inner voice that says you can't do this or that you're not strong enough. You've survived what the enemy meant for your destruction. You are stronger than you know. And God is giving you even more strength to pursue the healing he has for you. I can't promise it will be easy or give you a guarantee as to how long it will take or what the process will look like. But I can remind you that God has promised to never leave you or forsake you. Never. He's ready to walk with you on this journey toward healing and freedom. Are you ready?

Overcoming Anxiety

Anxiety

FOR THE PURPOSES of this book, I'm referring to a general state of anxiety or being anxious, not the diagnosed medical condition. If you feel that your anxiety is such that you need medical attention, please see your physician as the content here is not a replacement for medical care.

Most of us can become anxious about various matters from time to time. Fears of what might happen overwhelm us, and our stress level increases. Sometimes these fears are reasonable, and sometimes they are not. Regardless, we do not benefit by reacting from a place of fear or anxiety.

Possible Roots

Perfectionism can be a root of anxiety, causing you to become fearful of failure when faced with a new experience. If you have perfectionistic tendencies, you might find the set of blog posts on that topic helpful. They can be found beginning here.

Anxiety may also be the result of traumatic circumstances that you've experienced that have left you in a higher state of alertness or with greater fears of the future because of what's happened to you in the past.

Epigenetics is discovering that anxiety can also be a response to trauma experienced by your ancestors. This causes you to react to situations because of the trauma response hardwired into your DNA or your cellular memory.

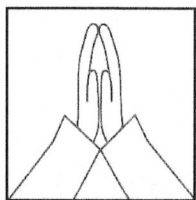

Father, I come before you this day because I need your help to access the freedom from anxiety. Jesus purchased for me on the cross. I take authority over myself, my space, and my will, and I submit myself to you and agree with you completely wherever you lead me through this process. I remove anything within myself that's hiding this issue and cut off all enemy access, placing everything into Jesus's hands. I ask you, Lord Jesus, to gather up and bind all warfare that would seek to hinder me from becoming free from anxiety or any other issue. Please send the angelic support I need.

I repent of all enemy rights and agreements and suspend them from all areas of access he has. I place them into Jesus's hands to keep during my work. Thank you, Father, for your provision and protection.

I ask you, Holy Spirit, for any blessings I need as I do this work. I ask for an anointing of power and authority as I address this issue. Please give me clarity of thought and intention and a breakthrough in healing. In Jesus's name. Amen.

Generational Issues

A PART OF MANY inner healing protocols and methods is a process that goes by different names. I use the phrase "generational work", but I've heard the terms ancestral cleansing and bloodline clearing, among others. As far as I know, these teachings are all based on the idea that the sins of our fathers (and mothers) can negatively impact us today.

You can see this most clearly when there is a strong family history of abuse or alcoholism. In fact, one scientific study shows that family members of alcoholics run three times the risk of alcohol abuse while for family members of other substance abusers, the risk is twice as high when compared with those who have no family history of alcohol abuse.[4]

Generational issues also manifest in a family history of poverty, anger, sexual, or even health issues. The theory is that when an ancestor started down that path, for whatever reason, their children, grandchildren, etc., carried on this destructive tradition. These issues might even be more subtle than the listed examples. For instance, overcoming an issue is much more difficult than it should be, and it's a constant battle to stay free. Maybe the people in

---

4 K. C. Pears, D. M. Capaldi, and L. D. Owen "Substance Use Risk Across Three Generations: The Roles of Parent Discipline Practices and Inhibitory Control," US National Library of Medicine National Institutes of Health, September 21, 2007, 21(3): 373–386. https://www.ncbi.nlm.nih.gov/pmc/articles/PMC1988842.

your bloodline are overweight, but you are not. But you struggle to maintain a healthy weight, for example.

I don't believe that all our sins are generational or affect the generations after us. But some clearly seem to. And the enemy is often at work in the middle of the mess. He is ever watching to catch us at our weakest. His job description is to steal, kill, and destroy, and he doesn't seem to ever go on vacation. (See John 10:10.)

Before I go any further, I want to emphasize that you are not held personally responsible for your ancestor's sin. You are only responsible for your own sins. But the generational piece adds a pressure or weight that increases the likelihood that you might sin in a particular area. We have a choice whether or not we enter into the sin, but even if we don't, the generational piece seems to make the fight against that sin more difficult than it needs to be.

The Process

1. What Are We Dealing with?

Pray and ask God to show you where anxiety started. Once you know the starting point, then it's easy. The enemy operates best in hiddenness and darkness. Once we know what we're dealing with, he doesn't stand much of a chance. Note: If you are adopted, then you have two sets of parents to potentially deal with. Since adoption is a physical and legal transaction, this seems to impact the spiritual realm as well.

2. Confession and Repentance

Identificational repentance clears the enemy's access to us because of generational issues. This means repenting on behalf of a larger group you're part of, in this case, your family. Again, you are not necessarily saying you are guilty of those sins, but you are standing in the gap for your family to remove the access the enemy has on you and your bloodline.

Nehemiah shows us this when he asked God to forgive "us" for the state of the walls of Jerusalem. He had nothing to do with the broken-down walls. You aren't saying you are guilty of the sin; you are saying you are sorry it happened and that the enemy has gained access to your bloodline because of it.

You then want to repent on your ancestor's behalf for committing this sin and allowing it access to your bloodline. (You do not need specific details about the sin.) Forgive them where appropriate. Then confess and repent on behalf of each generation from that time until now for not addressing this matter or for allowing it access. Also confess and repent of any way you have come into agreement with this sin, which removes the enemy's legal rights to our bloodline. We've already weakened its hold by releasing the negative emotions.

3. Eliminate the Warfare

Now that you have ended the enemy's rights, gather them up and cast them to the cross of Jesus. Revoke all rights to you and your bloodline and place the blood of Jesus between all that mess and all of your bloodline. Remember, you are doing this on behalf of all the descendants of that original person. I don't know how far out that reaches, but I am personally aware distant family members set free from migraines because one person addressed these issues. You have more influence than you think!

4. Input the Positive

We then release the opposite spirit of the demonic attack and all the good things of God that pertain to your life and to the lives of your family members and all those impacted by this generational issue. I pray from a logical standpoint. For instance, if with the issue relates to anger, I release love and peace, etc., but I also listen for the Spirit to lead. We want you and your bloodline to be full of the things of God.

We cannot control the choices that others make. You are not responsible for anyone's choices and behaviors but your own. But when you are under the weight of a generational piece, you don't know that you have another

choice. The removal of this dark cloud over your bloodline opens realms of possibilities to choose a better path. Breaking this generational issue doesn't mean that you never engage in the former behavior or thought process again although that can happen. But sometimes we need to walk out the matter and practice making better choices. Once you are free from the generational issue, it should be much easier than it was before.

The following is a sample prayer to walk through step-by-step, but this is also the perfect time to practice listening prayer. Only the Holy Spirit knows the full effects of this generational issue on your life, so listen carefully to his voice as you walk through this process and pray additional points as he leads you. Read through the prayer first and then make a note of anything the Holy Spirit wants you to add before you begin. You can also stop after each point, make notes, and then pray as you go.

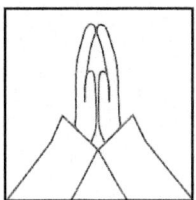

I confess that my ancestors committed the sin of anxiety, believing that what we do is our identity. Through this, they allowed the enemy access to their bloodline. I repent on each person's behalf for committing this sin and allowing the enemy access to us. I forgive them. I also confess and repent on behalf of myself and every other member of my bloodline who took part in the sin of anxiety, including associated sins of fear, perfectionism, worry, etc.

I forgive myself and all those in my bloodline who have committed the sin of anxiety or who have influenced me to take part in this sin and for the consequences of that sin in my life. (Specifically name anyone the Holy Spirit brings to your mind.)

I ask you to forgive me, Jesus, for agreeing with this issue and for committing these sins. I receive your forgiveness, and I forgive myself for taking part in this issue and for all the effects it has had on my life.

I revoke all agreements with anxiety on my behalf and as much as I can on behalf of all those in my bloodline. I revoke any agreements I or my family made with the entities of anxiety or any others affiliated with this or under their authority. I revoke all their rights to me and my entire bloodline past, present, and future from this time forward.

I gather up all these entities and agreements, and I cast them to the cross of Jesus. I place the blood of Jesus between all that and myself and my entire bloodline. I reverse and correct all the effects of anxiety in my life and in the lives of my family.

On behalf of my family, I receive the freedom Jesus Christ bought for me when he died on the cross and rose again, defeating all the works of the enemy. I receive his identity and courage and choose to listen to what he says about who I am. (This is an excellent time to pause and listen to what else God wants to give you. Write these down to meditate on later.)

You can do identificational repentance on behalf of any group you are a part of or identify with. It's not only your family. In all cases, you are not saying you have taken part in whatever it is you're repenting of. Instead, you can stand in the gap for the group at large because you are a part of the group. You can think in terms of culture, race, denomination, role in society, gender, position, occupation, etc. For example, I've done identificational repentance for clients on behalf of church leadership even though I wasn't a part of the church that hurt my client but because I have held positions of leadership within the church. You can use this powerful tool to set others free.

Generational Blessings

Generational issues not only pressure you to sin but also block the rightful inheritance the Lord has for your bloodline. Not only do I want you to be

free from the enemy's torment, but I also want you to be released into all the Lord has for you.

You may or may not know what your inheritance should have been. In either case, ask the Lord to reveal what the inheritance is to you and how you can access it. My book with Del Hungerford and Seneca Schurbon *Accessing Your Spiritual Inheritance,* covers this in much more depth than I can here. In short, ask God for dreams and visions and then ask him to go with you into those areas and follow his lead on what to do. This might be easier to do after you've completed all the steps in this book. So if you're struggling to understand inheritance, then make a note to return to this after you've finished the book.

Forgiveness

FORGIVENESS IS ONE of the major blockages to healing of all kinds. Holding unforgiveness toward yourself or others gives the enemy permission to torment you. You might have heard that unforgiveness is like drinking poison and expecting the other person to die.[5] It doesn't work. It also allows that person to live rent-free in your head.[6] Not a good idea!

Forgiveness is a process, however, and the larger the issue being forgiven, often the longer the process. The process, however begins with your willingness to forgive the person, God, or even yourself. Once you decide to forgive, remind yourself that you've decided to forgive, and move on again when those ugly feelings come back up,.

The process of forgiveness often depends on the degree of hurt that someone caused. The process can be lengthy, but doing the work is well worth it so that you are completely set free from whatever they did to hurt you. The decision to forgive is a one-time event; the process of forgiving can take years. It becomes easier the more you remind yourself of your decision to forgive, but you might have many layers to work through, depending on the effects these actions had in your life. Give yourself grace for this journey. It is well worth it!

---

5 Emmet Fox, The Sermon on the Mount (Houston: Harper & Brothers, 1938), 99.

6 Esther Lederer (Ann Landers), Wildmind Meditation, October 31. 2007, accessed April 27, 2019, https://www.wildmind.org/blogs/quote-of-the-month/ann-landers-resentment.

Often, the person we struggle the most to forgive is our self. Holding a grudge against yourself really does you no favors, however. Jesus forgives you freely. Please follow his example and forgive yourself freely as well.

I'm including two sample prayers. Please fill in the blanks as appropriate for you and your situation.

Forgiving Others

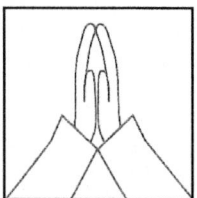

I forgive _____ for teaching me that my identity and worth was based on what I do and not who I am. (Repeat as needed and add what you're forgiving them for if needed.) I forgive all who have sinned against me and who have set me up to sin. I forgive all who have hurt me out of their own woundedness. I release them from all I feel they owe me, all judgements I've made against them, and all punishments I wanted them to experience. I replace any curses I've spoken against them with blessings. I release them into your hands, Father, and pray they would find healing from their wounds.

Forgiving Yourself

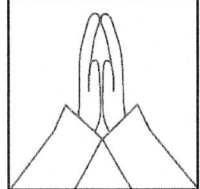

I forgive myself for believing the lies of anxiety because you forgave me. I forgive myself for hurting myself and others out of my woundedness. I release myself from all accusations or judgements and all hatred and slander I made against myself. I forgive myself for making mistakes and falling short of God's best for my life. I accept myself even as you accept me, Jesus, and I ask you to help me learn to love myself as you love me. I trust that, even as I accept myself where I am, you are at work to bring me to greater levels of wholeness and are recreating me into your image. I give myself grace for this process of becoming the person you created me to be.

I encourage you to do a Bible study and discover all the blessings that Christ has given you and who he says you are.

Ungodly Beliefs and Lies

G OD WANTS US to believe him and his Word. Our beliefs shape who we are and what we believe about ourselves, others, and God. Ungodly beliefs are contrary to the character of God and his Word. They are typically acquired from painful events you experience, from friends and family, and from your culture. They include lies such as,

- "There's no way I can handle this."
- "I am a victim of my circumstances."
- "I have no control over this anxiety."

Ungodly beliefs shape our experiences and behavior.

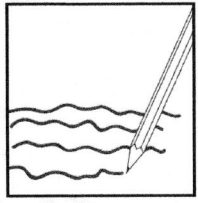

By replacing these ungodly beliefs with godly beliefs, we can reshape our experiences and behavior so that they align with what God says about us. Since ungodly beliefs are such a powerful force in our lives that shape our experiences, they are sometimes difficult for us to find on our own. You can

spot them when you are reading the Bible and you think what you read is not for you. That cynicism alerts you to an ungodly belief. You can also spend time in listening prayer, and ask God to share with you any false beliefs. If you struggle with this or can't spot the lie, seek help from a friend or trusted advisor.

Once you identify an ungodly belief or a lie about anxiety, work your way through the following prayer:

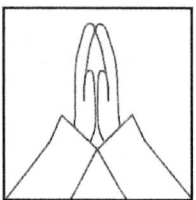

Father, I confess and repent for believing the lie that _____. I forgive any who contributed to the formation of this belief in me, specifically ____ (list whoever comes to mind). I ask you, Father to forgive me for believing this lie and for all the effects this lie has had in my life. Thank you for your forgiveness. Because you forgive me, I can forgive myself for believing this lie and for all the effects it has had in my life. I renounce the belief that _____, and I revoke all agreements made with the enemy related to this belief. I accept the truth that _____. (This is generally the opposite of the lie, but spend quiet time and allow the Lord to speak the truth he wants you to believe.)

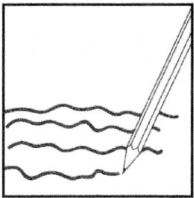

Write out the godly belief and read it aloud several times a day. Also search the Bible for verses reinforcing this new belief and personalize them. Write them out and read them aloud. Continue to do this until the truth saturates your being and shifts your behavior and experiences.

Word Curses

A WORD CURSE IS something negative said to you or about you that you believe and internalize so that it shapes your beliefs about yourself, your abilities, or your circumstances. Typically these also contribute to your failures in some way. You can also speak a word curse about yourself. Some common ones related to anxiety include:

- "I'll never be okay."
- "It will always be this bad."
- "I'm trapped in this cycle."
- "There is no hope for me."

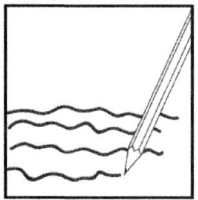

Spend time in prayer and allow the Holy Spirit to reveal any active curses that are impacting you. Once you identify any you have heard or said to yourself, you can break them off with the following prayer.

Father, I forgive _____ (this may be yourself), for cursing me by saying _____. (Repeat this for each of the people and curses you've written or what the Holy Spirit reveals to you as you pray.) I repent for believing this curse and for allowing it to shape my beliefs about myself, other people, my circumstances, and you. I ask for and receive your forgiveness. Thank you. I revoke and break all rights these curses had in my life and in my relationships and circumstances. I gather them up and cast them to the cross of Jesus along with any entities involved. I place the blood of Jesus between all that and me. I ask you, Jesus, to help me reverse and correct all the effects of these curses in my life, and help me appropriate the blessings you have for me in place of these curses. Thank you.

Soul Ties

SOUL TIES CAN be godly and healthy or ungodly. While sex is one way a soul tie forms, it is not the only way. We find godly soul ties in close, healthy relationships within healthy boundaries; those are beneficial, and we want to leave them alone or even strengthen them. Ungodly soul ties happen when two people make an inappropriate connection such as, a controlling or manipulative relationship that attempts to take away the free will of the other person. Not only does the ungodly soul tie give the other person more access to you than they should have, it also seems to give the enemy greater access to you.

I recommend praying to break any ungodly soul ties with anyone who comes to mind. If you have no soul ties with that person, then nothing happens, but you do have soul ties with them, then it's best to break them. You might have both godly and ungodly soul ties with the same person, especially your spouse or close family. Therefore, we specify we are breaking the ungodly soul ties.

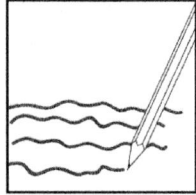

You can ask God for a list of people before you pray or just mention those that come to mind as you pray. You don't need to try to think of anyone and everyone. Just go with whoever immediately comes to mind and then move on. If God reminds you of others later, you can come back and pray again.

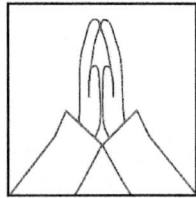

Father, I confess and repent of any ungodly soul ties I have with ___. I forgive ___ for their part in creating these soul ties. (Repeat for each person who comes to mind.) I take back what they have that is rightfully mine, and I send back to them what I have that is rightfully theirs, washed in the blood of Jesus and sent with a message of salvation, healing, and a blessing. I break off these soul ties. I seal up the connection point with the blood of Jesus. I revoke any rights the enemy has gained to me through these soul ties, and I gather up all entities involved and cast them to the cross of Jesus. I place the blood of Jesus between all that and me. In Jesus's name. Amen.

Emotional Wounds

ONE OF THE major access points the enemy has to each of us is through unhealed or ineffectively healed emotional wounds. We are hurt many times throughout our lives, but we can handle these hurts in a healthy or unhealthy manner. Sometimes these hurts shape our beliefs about ourselves and others inaccurately. Maybe the person disregarded our feelings, or no one knew how to help us work through what we thought, felt, or experienced. There's probably no end to the various ways people can hurt us. But do we allow God to help us work through those hurts, or do we stuff them, hoping they will go away?

Before we continue, I believe most people do the best they can with what they know: both we who hurt and the ones who are doing the hurting. Most people act in hurtful ways because of their own woundings. Most people are doing the best they know how given what they've been through. And this is one of the most important reasons for finding healing so that the pattern of hurting others ends with us. We get healed, and we learn how to treat others better, and the world becomes a better place.

In some cases, you might need someone else to help walk you through this process so that you don't become stuck and can keep moving. This depends on how healed you are, how fresh or how deep the wound is, current triggers related to the issue, etc. If you become stuck, this is a perfect time to phone a

friend, or seek a minister who can help you navigate this process. There is no shame in seeking help. The point is to get healed!

I recommend you take one memory or hurt at a time and go through the process. If more than one occasion of the same hurt comes to mind, you can often deal with them as a group. Just set your intention to include each incident that hurt occurred in your life. If you have different incidents, make a note of the others, and pick one to start with. You can keep going through your list until they are all done although you might need to take time for your system to recover after each of them. Again, this depends on how the hurts affected you.

The following is a basic template I use during sessions with clients. It is a guide, not a super rigid framework. This order is generally best because I've found it to be the most effective. But sometimes you need to go back to an earlier point and then move forward.

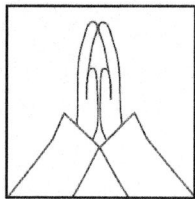

1. Ask Jesus or the Holy Spirit to take you to the first memory of hurt related to anxiety.
2. Tell Jesus how you are feeling in that memory.
3. Give all those negative emotions to Jesus. Some people find it helpful to picture pulling the negativity out of each cell or body part, starting at the toes and working upward, finally giving it all to Jesus or placing it at the foot of the cross. Sometimes you need to take each emotion, one at a time, and give it to Jesus. Other times, you can gather up the whole mess at once and give it to him. Keep doing this until you've given it all to him or placed it all at the cross.
4. Place the blood of Jesus between all the negativity and you. Ask Jesus to fill you with the opposite of what you've just released, e.g., his patience, love, hope, belonging, etc.

5. Invite Jesus into the memory to heal your hurt. Watch and wait to see what he does. He might want to take you to the Father.

6. You might need to revisit some earlier chapters and walk through forgiveness, ungodly lies and beliefs, etc.

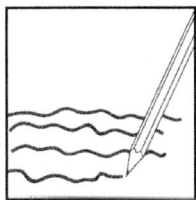

7. When you've finished all the healing, ask Jesus, Father, or the Holy Spirit to tell you what he thinks of you or of the situation as appropriate. Write what you see, hear, feel, or sense.

You can repeat this process for all hurts related to anxiety or any other issue you're dealing with. This is also effective for current hurts.

Demonic Oppression

I'VE OFTEN HEARD the demonic described as rats feeding on garbage. Part of what we've been doing so far in this book is getting rid of the garbage of anxiety so that the rats have nothing left to attach to or feed on. Little by little, we've eliminated the contact points or rights we've given the enemy. Once we heal, break, and close off their rights, access, and contact points, we can easily kick them off.

We usually name the demonic by their function. Since we've been dealing with anxiety, we will get rid of the demons of anxiety and any under their authority or involved with them. Sometimes you can just toss the whole package, and sometimes you need to specifically name them one by one. Just repeat the prayer as often as you need to until you've eliminated them all. If you think of others later, just pray through the prayer again.

You'll notice this is not a complicated prayer. It's simple but powerful. Through Christ, you have authority over the enemy, especially when you've removed any rights the enemy has to be there. This is a legal proceeding not a power play, so volume is unnecessary. The enemy is not hearing-impaired, and he knows better than we do the authority we carry. So he often relies on hiddenness, darkness, and intimidation. But we've seen his plan and foiled his plots, so let's kick him out!

1. Father, forgive me for buying into the lies of anxiety, for giving anxiety access to my life through all the generational issues, soul ties, unforgiveness, ungodly beliefs, word curses, and woundings.
2. I forgive myself for buying into the lies of anxiety, and I accept your forgiveness.
3. I renounce, break, and cancel all agreements made with anxiety along with any other entity under its authority or affiliated with it. (Name any that come to mind, but don't linger here.)
4. I gather up anxiety and all entities involved in any way (including the list in #3 as needed) and cast them to the cross of Jesus. I place the blood of Jesus between all that and me.
5. I ask you, Jesus, to fill me with your peace and wholeness (and the opposite of the entities you've mentioned). Please teach me how to walk in your ____ as I move forward in my life.

Overcoming Insecurity

Insecurity

INSECURITY USUALLY COMES in a couple different ways. One is a form of self-consciousness—not knowing how people will respond to us or what they will think of us or feeling less than or not good enough. The other is a lack of feeling safe. This can be emotional, but it can also be a lack of physical safety, such as fear of abuse or victimization, but also not knowing if you'll have what you need to survive: food, shelter, clothing, etc.

You might want to go through the following lists at least twice, thinking of the different manifestations you see in your life each time.

Possible Roots

Trauma plays a significant role in nearly all cases here. But as has been shown through epigenetics, the trauma may not have been yours; your ancestors could have experienced it. For example, The Great Depression, The Holocaust, The Potato Famine, and other similar events have all been shown to leave genetic traces of trauma in the descendants of those who experienced them, even though they weren't born yet.

Of course, your own personal trauma can leave its mark. People who, as children, grow up in homes where there was never enough food may be compulsive overeaters as they still carry the insecurity of wondering if there will be enough food. People who have been repeatedly or significantly ridiculed may always worry that others will do the same.

Unusual Presentations

As with many traumas, people tend to react at opposite extremes. Some may be very self-effacing; others may become arrogant. Some may carefully ration their food or clothing while others eat excessively or purchase items to feel safer. The behaviors may differ greatly while the root is still the same.

Father, I come before you this day because I need your help to access the freedom from insecurity. Jesus purchased for me on the cross. I take authority over myself, my space, and my will, and I submit myself to you and agree with you completely wherever you lead me through this process. I remove anything within myself that's hiding this issue and cut off all enemy access, placing everything into Jesus's hands. I ask you, Lord Jesus, to gather up and bind all warfare that would seek to hinder me from becoming free from insecurity or any other issue. Please send the angelic support I need.

I repent of all enemy rights and agreements and suspend them from all areas of access he has. I place them into Jesus's hands to keep during my work. Thank you, Father, for your provision and protection.

I ask you, Holy Spirit, for any blessings I need as I do this work. I ask for an anointing of power and authority as I address this issue. Please give me clarity of thought and intention and a breakthrough in healing. In Jesus's name. Amen.

Generational Issues

A PART OF MANY inner healing protocols and methods is a process that goes by different names. I use the phrase "generational work", but I've heard the terms ancestral cleansing and bloodline clearing, among others. As far as I know, these teachings are all based on the idea that the sins of our fathers (and mothers) can negatively impact us today.

You can see this most clearly when there is a strong family history of abuse or alcoholism. In fact, one scientific study shows that family members of alcoholics run three times the risk of alcohol abuse while for family members of other substance abusers, the risk is twice as high when compared with those who have no family history of alcohol abuse.[7]

Generational issues also manifest in a family history of poverty, anger, sexual, or even health issues. The theory is that when an ancestor started down that path, for whatever reason, their children, grandchildren, etc., carried on this destructive tradition. These issues might even be more subtle than the listed examples. For instance, overcoming an issue is much more difficult than it should be, and it's a constant battle to stay free. Maybe the people in

---

7 K. C. Pears, D. M. Capaldi, and L. D. Owen "Substance Use Risk Across Three Generations: The Roles of Parent Discipline Practices and Inhibitory Control," US National Library of Medicine National Institutes of Health, September 21, 2007, 21(3): 373–386. https://www.ncbi.nlm.nih.gov/pmc/articles/PMC1988842.

your bloodline are overweight, but you are not. But you struggle to maintain a healthy weight, for example.

I don't believe that all our sins are generational or affect the generations after us. But some clearly seem to. And the enemy is often at work in the middle of the mess. He is ever watching to catch us at our weakest. His job description is to steal, kill, and destroy, and he doesn't seem to ever go on vacation. (See John 10:10.)

Before I go any further, I want to emphasize that you are not held personally responsible for your ancestor's sin. You are only responsible for your own sins. But the generational piece adds a pressure or weight that increases the likelihood that you might sin in a particular area. We have a choice whether or not we enter into the sin, but even if we don't, the generational piece seems to make the fight against that sin more difficult than it needs to be.

The Process

1. What Are We Dealing with?

Pray and ask God to show you where insecurity started. Once you know the starting point, then it's easy. The enemy operates best in hiddenness and darkness. Once we know what we're dealing with, he doesn't stand much of a chance. Note: If you are adopted, then you have two sets of parents to potentially deal with. Since adoption is a physical and legal transaction, this seems to impact the spiritual realm as well.

2. Confession and Repentance

Identificational repentance clears the enemy's access to us because of generational issues. This means repenting on behalf of a larger group you're part of, in this case, your family. Again, you are not necessarily saying you are guilty of those sins, but you are standing in the gap for your family to remove the access the enemy has on you and your bloodline.

Nehemiah shows us this when he asked God to forgive "us" for the state of the walls of Jerusalem. He had nothing to do with the broken-down walls. You aren't saying you are guilty of the sin; you are saying you are sorry it happened and that the enemy has gained access to your bloodline because of it.

You then want to repent on your ancestor's behalf for committing this sin and allowing it access to your bloodline. (You do not need specific details about the sin.) Forgive them where appropriate. Then confess and repent on behalf of each generation from that time until now for not addressing this matter or for allowing it access. Also confess and repent of any way you have come into agreement with this sin, which removes the enemy's legal rights to our bloodline. We've already weakened its hold by releasing the negative emotions.

3. Eliminate the Warfare

Now that you have ended the enemy's rights, gather them up and cast them to the cross of Jesus. Revoke all rights to you and your bloodline and place the blood of Jesus between all that mess and all of your bloodline. Remember, you are doing this on behalf of all the descendants of that original person. I don't know how far out that reaches, but I am personally aware distant family members set free from migraines because one person addressed these issues. You have more influence than you think!

4. Input the Positive

We then release the opposite spirit of the demonic attack and all the good things of God that pertain to your life and to the lives of your family members and all those impacted by this generational issue. I pray from a logical standpoint. For instance, if with the issue relates to anger, I release love and peace, etc., but I also listen for the Spirit to lead. We want you and your bloodline to be full of the things of God.

We cannot control the choices that others make. You are not responsible for anyone's choices and behaviors but your own. But when you are under the weight of a generational piece, you don't know that you have another

choice. The removal of this dark cloud over your bloodline opens realms of possibilities to choose a better path. Breaking this generational issue doesn't mean that you never engage in the former behavior or thought process again although that can happen. But sometimes we need to walk out the matter and practice making better choices. Once you are free from the generational issue, it should be much easier than it was before.

The following is a sample prayer to walk through step-by-step, but this is also the perfect time to practice listening prayer. Only the Holy Spirit knows the full effects of this generational issue on your life, so listen carefully to his voice as you walk through this process and pray additional points as he leads you. Read through the prayer first and then make a note of anything the Holy Spirit wants you to add before you begin. You can also stop after each point, make notes, and then pray as you go.

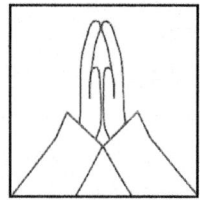

1. I confess that my ancestors came into agreement with insecurity, believing that what we do is our identity. Through this, they allowed the enemy access to their bloodline. I repent on each person's behalf for committing this sin and allowing the enemy access to us. I forgive them. I also confess and repent on behalf of myself and every other member of my bloodline who came into agreement with insecurity, including associated sins or agreements of fear, self-consciousness, overeating, hoarding, etc.

2. I forgive myself and all those in my bloodline who have committed the sin of insecurity or who have influenced me to take part in this sin and for the consequences of that sin in my life. (Specifically name anyone the Holy Spirit brings to your mind.)

3. I ask you to forgive me, Jesus, for agreeing with this issue and for committing these sins. I receive your forgiveness, and I forgive myself for taking part in this issue and for all the effects it has had on my life.

4. I revoke all agreements with insecurity on my behalf and as much as I can on behalf of all those in my bloodline. I revoke any agreements I or my family made with the entities of insecurity or any others affiliated with this or under their authority. I revoke all their rights to me and my entire bloodline past, present, and future from this time forward.

5. I gather up all these entities and agreements, and I cast them to the cross of Jesus. I place the blood of Jesus between all that and myself and my entire bloodline. I reverse and correct all the effects of insecurity in my life and in the lives of my family.

6. On behalf of my family, I receive the freedom Jesus Christ bought for me when he died on the cross and rose again, defeating all the works of the enemy. I receive his identity and courage and choose to listen to what he says about who I am. (This is an excellent time to pause and listen to what else God wants to give you. Write these down to meditate on later.)

You can do identificational repentance on behalf of any group you are a part of or identify with. It's not only your family. In all cases, you are not saying you have taken part in whatever it is you're repenting of. Instead, you can stand in the gap for the group at large because you are a part of the group. You can think in terms of culture, race, denomination, role in society, gender, position, occupation, etc. For example, I've done identificational repentance for clients on behalf of church leadership even though I wasn't a part of the church that hurt my client but because I have held positions of leadership within the church. You can use this powerful tool to set others free.

Generational Blessings

Generational issues not only pressure you to sin but also block the rightful inheritance the Lord has for your bloodline. Not only do I want you to be free from the enemy's torment, but I also want you to be released into all the Lord has for you.

You may or may not know what your inheritance should have been. In either case, ask the Lord to reveal what the inheritance is to you and how you can access it. My book with Del Hungerford and Seneca Schurbon *Accessing Your Spiritual Inheritance,* covers this in much more depth than I can here. In short, ask God for dreams and visions and then ask him to go with you into those areas and follow his lead on what to do. This might be easier to do after you've completed all the steps in this book. So if you're struggling to understand inheritance, then make a note to return to this after you've finished the book.

Forgiveness

FORGIVENESS IS ONE of the major blockages to healing of all kinds. Holding unforgiveness toward yourself or others gives the enemy permission to torment you. You might have heard that unforgiveness is like drinking poison and expecting the other person to die.[8] It doesn't work. It also allows that person to live rent-free in your head.[9] Not a good idea!

Forgiveness is a process, however, and the larger the issue being forgiven, often the longer the process. The process, however begins with your willingness to forgive the person, God, or even yourself. Once you decide to forgive, remind yourself that you've decided to forgive, and move on again when those ugly feelings come back up,.

The process of forgiveness often depends on the degree of hurt that someone caused. The process can be lengthy, but doing the work is well worth it so that you are completely set free from whatever they did to hurt you. The decision to forgive is a one-time event; the process of forgiving can take years. It becomes easier the more you remind yourself of your decision to forgive, but you might have many layers to work through, depending on the effects these actions had in your life. Give yourself grace for this journey. It is well worth it!

---

8 Emmet Fox, The Sermon on the Mount (Houston: Harper & Brothers, 1938), 99.
9 Esther Lederer (Ann Landers), Wildmind Meditation, October 31. 2007, accessed April 27, 2019, https://www.wildmind.org/blogs/quote-of-the-month/ann-landers-resentment.

Often, the person we struggle the most to forgive is our self. Holding a grudge against yourself really does you no favors, however. Jesus forgives you freely. Please follow his example and forgive yourself freely as well.

I'm including two sample prayers. Please fill in the blanks as appropriate for you and your situation.

Forgiving Others

I forgive _____ for teaching me that my identity and worth was based on what I do and not who I am. (Repeat as needed and add what you're forgiving them for if needed.) I forgive all who have sinned against me and who have set me up to sin. I forgive all who have hurt me out of their own woundedness. I release them from all I feel they owe me, all judgements I've made against them, and all punishments I wanted them to experience. I replace any curses I've spoken against them with blessings. I release them into your hands, Father, and pray they would find healing from their wounds.

Forgiving Yourself

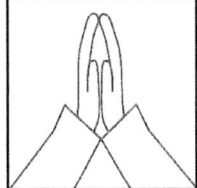

I forgive myself for believing the lies of insecurity because you forgave me. I forgive myself for hurting myself and others out of my woundedness. I release myself from all accusations or judgements and all hatred and slander I made against myself. I forgive myself for making mistakes and falling short of God's best for my life. I accept myself even as you accept me, Jesus, and I ask you to help me learn to love myself as you love me. I trust that, even as I accept myself where I am, you are at work to bring me to greater levels of wholeness and are recreating me into your image. I give myself grace for this process of becoming the person you created me to be.

I encourage you to do a Bible study and discover all the blessings that Christ has given you and who he says you are.

Ungodly Beliefs and Lies

G OD WANTS US to believe him and his Word. Our beliefs shape who we are and what we believe about ourselves, others, and God. Ungodly beliefs are contrary to the character of God and his Word. They are typically acquired from painful events you experience, from friends and family, and from your culture. They include lies such as,

- "There's no way I can trust these people."
- "I am never going to be safe."
- "I will never be accepted for who I am."

Ungodly beliefs shape our experiences and behavior.

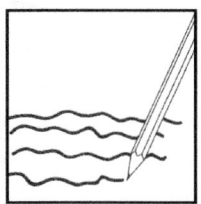

By replacing these ungodly beliefs with godly beliefs, we can reshape our experiences and behavior so that they align with what God says about us. Since ungodly beliefs are such a powerful force in our lives that shape our experiences, they are sometimes difficult for us to find on our own. You can

spot them when you are reading the Bible and you think what you read is not for you. That cynicism alerts you to an ungodly belief. You can also spend time in listening prayer, and ask God to share with you any false beliefs. If you struggle with this or can't spot the lie, seek help from a friend or trusted advisor.

Once you identify an ungodly belief or a lie about insecurity, work your way through the following prayer:

Father, I confess and repent for believing the lie that _____. I forgive any who contributed to the formation of this belief in me, specifically _____ (list whoever comes to mind). I ask you, Father to forgive me for believing this lie and for all the effects this lie has had in my life. Thank you for your forgiveness. Because you forgive me, I can forgive myself for believing this lie and for all the effects it has had in my life. I renounce the belief that _____, and I revoke all agreements made with the enemy related to this belief. I accept the truth that _____. (This is generally the opposite of the lie, but spend quiet time and allow the Lord to speak the truth he wants you to believe.)

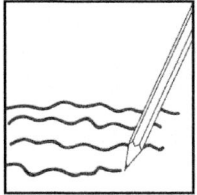

Write out the godly belief and read it aloud several times a day. Also search the Bible for verses reinforcing this new belief and personalize them. Write them out and read them aloud. Continue to do this until the truth saturates your being and shifts your behavior and experiences.

Word Curses

A WORD CURSE IS something negative said to you or about you that you believe and internalize so that it shapes your beliefs about yourself, your abilities, or your circumstances. Typically these also contribute to your failures in some way. You can also speak a word curse about yourself. Some common ones related to insecurity include:

- I'm not good enough, or good enough for _____.
- I'm too ___ (stupid, awkward, etc.).
- I'm not safe or secure.

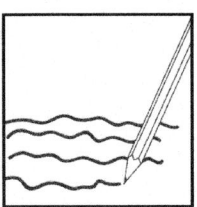

Spend time in prayer and allow the Holy Spirit to reveal any active curses that are impacting you. Once you identify any you have heard or said to yourself, you can break them off with the following prayer.

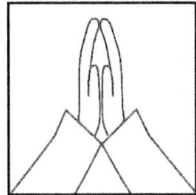

Father, I forgive _____ (this may be yourself), for cursing me by saying _____. (Repeat this for each of the people and curses you've written or what the Holy Spirit reveals to you as you pray.) I repent for believing this curse and for allowing it to shape my beliefs about myself, other people, my circumstances, and you. I ask for and receive your forgiveness. Thank you. I revoke and break all rights these curses had in my life and in my relationships and circumstances. I gather them up and cast them to the cross of Jesus along with any entities involved. I place the blood of Jesus between all that and me. I ask you, Jesus, to help me reverse and correct all the effects of these curses in my life, and help me appropriate the blessings you have for me in place of these curses. Thank you.

Soul Ties

SOUL TIES CAN be godly and healthy or ungodly. While sex is one way a soul tie forms, it is not the only way. We find godly soul ties in close, healthy relationships within healthy boundaries; those are beneficial, and we want to leave them alone or even strengthen them. Ungodly soul ties happen when two people make an inappropriate connection such as, a controlling or manipulative relationship that attempts to take away the free will of the other person. Not only does the ungodly soul tie give the other person more access to you than they should have, it also seems to give the enemy greater access to you.

I recommend praying to break any ungodly soul ties with anyone who comes to mind. If you have no soul ties with that person, then nothing happens, but you do have soul ties with them, then it's best to break them. You might have both godly and ungodly soul ties with the same person, especially your spouse or close family. Therefore, we specify we are breaking the ungodly soul ties.

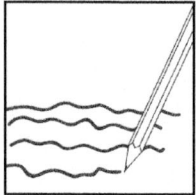

You can ask God for a list of people before you pray or just mention those that come to mind as you pray. You don't need to try to think of anyone and everyone. Just go with whoever immediately comes to mind and then move on. If God reminds you of others later, you can come back and pray again.

Father, I confess and repent of any ungodly soul ties I have with ___. I forgive ___ for their part in creating these soul ties. (Repeat for each person who comes to mind.) I take back what they have that is rightfully mine, and I send back to them what I have that is rightfully theirs, washed in the blood of Jesus and sent with a message of salvation, healing, and a blessing. I break off these soul ties. I seal up the connection point with the blood of Jesus. I revoke any rights the enemy has gained to me through these soul ties, and I gather up all entities involved and cast them to the cross of Jesus. I place the blood of Jesus between all that and me. In Jesus's name. Amen.

Emotional Wounds

O NE OF THE major access points the enemy has to each of us is through unhealed or ineffectively healed emotional wounds. We are hurt many times throughout our lives, but we can handle these hurts in a healthy or unhealthy manner. Sometimes these hurts shape our beliefs about ourselves and others inaccurately. Maybe the person disregarded our feelings, or no one knew how to help us work through what we thought, felt, or experienced. There's probably no end to the various ways people can hurt us. But do we allow God to help us work through those hurts, or do we stuff them, hoping they will go away?

Before we continue, I believe most people do the best they can with what they know: both we who hurt and the ones who are doing the hurting. Most people act in hurtful ways because of their own woundings. Most people are doing the best they know how given what they've been through. And this is one of the most important reasons for finding healing so that the pattern of hurting others ends with us. We get healed, and we learn how to treat others better, and the world becomes a better place.

In some cases, you might need someone else to help walk you through this process so that you don't become stuck and can keep moving. This depends on how healed you are, how fresh or how deep the wound is, current triggers related to the issue, etc. If you become stuck, this is a perfect time to phone a

friend, or seek a minister who can help you navigate this process. There is no shame in seeking help. The point is to get healed!

I recommend you take one memory or hurt at a time and go through the process. If more than one occasion of the same hurt comes to mind, you can often deal with them as a group. Just set your intention to include each incident that hurt occurred in your life. If you have different incidents, make a note of the others, and pick one to start with. You can keep going through your list until they are all done although you might need to take time for your system to recover after each of them. Again, this depends on how the hurts affected you.

The following is a basic template I use during sessions with clients. It is a guide, not a super rigid framework. This order is generally best because I've found it to be the most effective. But sometimes you need to go back to an earlier point and then move forward.

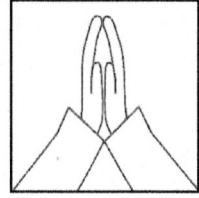

1. Ask Jesus or the Holy Spirit to take you to the first memory of hurt related to insecurity.
2. Tell Jesus how you are feeling in that memory.
3. Give all those negative emotions to Jesus. Some people find it helpful to picture pulling the negativity out of each cell or body part, starting at the toes and working upward, finally giving it all to Jesus or placing it at the foot of the cross. Sometimes you need to take each emotion, one at a time, and give it to Jesus. Other times, you can gather up the whole mess at once and give it to him. Keep doing this until you've given it all to him or placed it all at the cross.
4. Place the blood of Jesus between all the negativity and you. Ask Jesus to fill you with the opposite of what you've just released, e.g., his patience, love, hope, belonging, etc.

5. Invite Jesus into the memory to heal your hurt. Watch and wait to see what he does. He might want to take you to the Father.

6. You might need to revisit some earlier chapters and walk through forgiveness, ungodly lies and beliefs, etc.

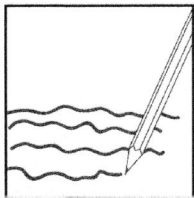

7. When you've finished all the healing, ask Jesus, Father, or the Holy Spirit to tell you what he thinks of you or of the situation as appropriate. Write what you see, hear, feel, or sense.

You can repeat this process for all hurts related to insecurity or any other issue you're dealing with. This is also effective for current hurts.

Demonic Oppression

I'VE OFTEN HEARD the demonic described as rats feeding on garbage. Part of what we've been doing so far in this book is getting rid of the garbage of insecurity so that the rats have nothing left to attach to or feed on. Little by little, we've eliminated the contact points or rights we've given the enemy. Once we heal, break, and close off their rights, access, and contact points, we can easily kick them off.

We usually name the demonic by their function. Since we've been dealing with insecurity, we will get rid of the demons of insecurity and any under their authority or involved with them. Sometimes you can just toss the whole package, and sometimes you need to specifically name them one by one. Just repeat the prayer as often as you need to until you've eliminated them all. If you think of others later, just pray through the prayer again.

You'll notice this is not a complicated prayer. It's simple but powerful. Through Christ, you have authority over the enemy, especially when you've removed any rights the enemy has to be there. This is a legal proceeding not a power play, so volume is unnecessary. The enemy is not hearing-impaired, and he knows better than we do the authority we carry. So he often relies on hiddenness, darkness, and intimidation. But we've seen his plan and foiled his plots, so let's kick him out!

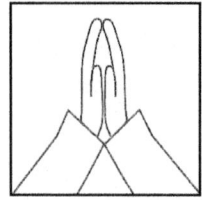

1. Father, forgive me for buying into the lies of insecurity, for giving insecurity access to my life through all the generational issues, soul ties, unforgiveness, ungodly beliefs, word curses, and woundings.

2. I forgive myself for buying into the lies of insecurity, and I accept your forgiveness.

3. I renounce, break, and cancel all agreements made with insecurity along with any other entity under its authority or affiliated with it. (Name any that come to mind, but don't linger here.)

4. I gather up insecurity and all entities involved in any way (including the list in #3 as needed) and cast them to the cross of Jesus. I place the blood of Jesus between all that and me.

5. I ask you, Jesus, to fill me with your peace and wholeness (and the opposite of the entities you've mentioned). Please teach me how to walk in your ____ as I move forward in my life.

Overcoming Control

Control

CONTROL HAS MANY facets. You can be controlled by outside forces or by people, you can be controlling of outside forces or of people—or at least attempt to control these, and/or you can be controlling of yourself.

Often, either we or others don't understand who we really are and so try and squish ourselves into a mold that they—or we!—do understand. Creatives are often pressured to be something or someone other than what they are, but they are certainly not the only group of people this applies to. For some, these expectations relate to gender or gender stereotypes.

Control may be an unwillingness to allow yourself to feel pain or frustration, so you carefully control your experiences to avoid those triggers or situations that cause you to face these things.

Some companies, churches, organizations, and more hold to a very strict and oppressive code of conduct and expectations for their employees or members.

Control can also be quite subtle, especially in the realm of prayer. If you're praying for someone—or they are praying for you—to do something in particular, then those prayers might be an attempt to control. Manipulation and control is from the dark side, and if you are going there, you've left the path of wisdom and truth. Be careful how and what you pray or allow to be prayed over you.

Possible Roots

Unhealthy anger is often a generational issue. Most people who are controlled seem to be controlled by people who have been controlled. This may be because of a huge variety of factors.

If you are very controlling of yourself, you may have possibly been controlled and learned that staying in that confined space was the only safe thing to do.

Either way, a lot of trauma often needs to be worked through from the past and present so that you can press into your future.

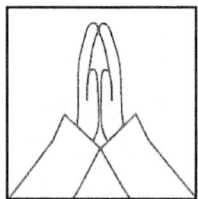

Father, I come before you this day because I need your help to access the freedom from control. Jesus purchased for me on the cross. I take authority over myself, my space, and my will, and I submit myself to you and agree with you completely wherever you lead me through this process. I remove anything within myself that's hiding this issue and cut off all enemy access, placing everything into Jesus's hands. I ask you, Lord Jesus, to gather up and bind all warfare that would seek to hinder me from becoming free from control or any other issue. Please send the angelic support I need.

I repent of all enemy rights and agreements and suspend them from all areas of access he has. I place them into Jesus's hands to keep during my work. Thank you, Father, for your provision and protection.

I ask you, Holy Spirit, for any blessings I need as I do this work. I ask for an anointing of power and authority as I address this issue. Please give me clarity of thought and intention and a breakthrough in healing. In Jesus's name. Amen.

Generational Issues

APART OF MANY inner healing protocols and methods is a process that goes by different names. I use the phrase "generational work", but I've heard the terms ancestral cleansing and bloodline clearing, among others. As far as I know, these teachings are all based on the idea that the sins of our fathers (and mothers) can negatively impact us today.

You can see this most clearly when there is a strong family history of abuse or alcoholism. In fact, one scientific study shows that family members of alcoholics run three times the risk of alcohol abuse while for family members of other substance abusers, the risk is twice as high when compared with those who have no family history of alcohol abuse.[10]

Generational issues also manifest in a family history of poverty, anger, sexual, or even health issues. The theory is that when an ancestor started down that path, for whatever reason, their children, grandchildren, etc., carried on this destructive tradition. These issues might even be more subtle than the listed examples. For instance, overcoming an issue is much more difficult than it should be, and it's a constant battle to stay free. Maybe the people in

---

10 K. C. Pears, D. M. Capaldi, and L. D. Owen "Substance Use Risk Across Three Generations: The Roles of Parent Discipline Practices and Inhibitory Control," US National Library of Medicine National Institutes of Health, September 21, 2007, 21(3): 373–386. https://www.ncbi.nlm.nih.gov/pmc/articles/PMC1988842.

your bloodline are overweight, but you are not. But you struggle to maintain a healthy weight, for example.

I don't believe that all our sins are generational or affect the generations after us. But some clearly seem to. And the enemy is often at work in the middle of the mess. He is ever watching to catch us at our weakest. His job description is to steal, kill, and destroy, and he doesn't seem to ever go on vacation. (See John 10:10.)

Before I go any further, I want to emphasize that you are not held personally responsible for your ancestor's sin. You are only responsible for your own sins. But the generational piece adds a pressure or weight that increases the likelihood that you might sin in a particular area. We have a choice whether or not we enter into the sin, but even if we don't, the generational piece seems to make the fight against that sin more difficult than it needs to be.

The Process

1. What Are We Dealing with?

Pray and ask God to show you where control started. Once you know the starting point, then it's easy. The enemy operates best in hiddenness and darkness. Once we know what we're dealing with, he doesn't stand much of a chance. Note: If you are adopted, then you have two sets of parents to potentially deal with. Since adoption is a physical and legal transaction, this seems to impact the spiritual realm as well.

2. Confession and Repentance

Identificational repentance clears the enemy's access to us because of generational issues. This means repenting on behalf of a larger group you're part of, in this case, your family. Again, you are not necessarily saying you are guilty of those sins, but you are standing in the gap for your family to remove the access the enemy has on you and your bloodline.

Nehemiah shows us this when he asked God to forgive "us" for the state of the walls of Jerusalem. He had nothing to do with the broken-down walls. You aren't saying you are guilty of the sin; you are saying you are sorry it happened and that the enemy has gained access to your bloodline because of it.

You then want to repent on your ancestor's behalf for committing this sin and allowing it access to your bloodline. (You do not need specific details about the sin.) Forgive them where appropriate. Then confess and repent on behalf of each generation from that time until now for not addressing this matter or for allowing it access. Also confess and repent of any way you have come into agreement with this sin, which removes the enemy's legal rights to our bloodline. We've already weakened its hold by releasing the negative emotions.

3. Eliminate the Warfare

Now that you have ended the enemy's rights, gather them up and cast them to the cross of Jesus. Revoke all rights to you and your bloodline and place the blood of Jesus between all that mess and all of your bloodline. Remember, you are doing this on behalf of all the descendants of that original person. I don't know how far out that reaches, but I am personally aware distant family members set free from migraines because one person addressed these issues. You have more influence than you think!

4. Input the Positive

We then release the opposite spirit of the demonic attack and all the good things of God that pertain to your life and to the lives of your family members and all those impacted by this generational issue. I pray from a logical standpoint. For instance, if with the issue relates to anger, I release love and peace, etc., but I also listen for the Spirit to lead. We want you and your bloodline to be full of the things of God.

We cannot control the choices that others make. You are not responsible for anyone's choices and behaviors but your own. But when you are under the weight of a generational piece, you don't know that you have another choice. The removal of this dark cloud over your bloodline opens realms of possibilities to choose a better path. Breaking this generational issue doesn't mean that you never engage in the former behavior or thought process again although that can happen. But sometimes we need to walk out the matter and practice making better choices. Once you are free from the generational issue, it should be much easier than it was before.

The following is a sample prayer to walk through step-by-step, but this is also the perfect time to practice listening prayer. Only the Holy Spirit knows the full effects of this generational issue on your life, so listen carefully to his voice as you walk through this process and pray additional points as he leads you. Read through the prayer first and then make a note of anything the Holy Spirit wants you to add before you begin. You can also stop after each point, make notes, and then pray as you go.

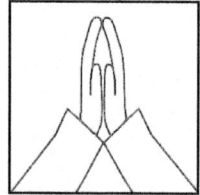

1. I confess that my ancestors came into agreement with control, believing that what we do is our identity. Through this, they allowed the enemy access to their bloodline. I repent on each person's behalf for committing this sin and allowing the enemy access to us. I forgive them. I also confess and repent on behalf of myself and every other member of my bloodline who came into agreement with control, including associated sins or agreements of control, manipulation, fear, and an orphan mentality, etc.

2. I forgive myself and all those in my bloodline who have committed the sin of control or who have influenced me to take part in this sin and for the consequences of that sin in my life. (Specifically name anyone the Holy Spirit brings to your mind.)

3. I ask you to forgive me, Jesus, for agreeing with this issue and for committing these sins. I receive your forgiveness, and I forgive myself for taking part in this issue and for all the effects it has had on my life.

4. I revoke all agreements with control on my behalf and as much as I can on behalf of all those in my bloodline. I revoke any agreements I or my family made with the entities of control or any others affiliated with this or under their authority. I revoke all their rights to me and my entire bloodline past, present, and future from this time forward.

5. I gather up all these entities and agreements, and I cast them to the cross of Jesus. I place the blood of Jesus between all that and myself and my entire bloodline. I reverse and correct all the effects of control in my life and in the lives of my family.

6. On behalf of my family, I receive the freedom Jesus Christ bought for me when he died on the cross and rose again, defeating all the works of the enemy. I receive his identity and courage and choose to listen to what he says about who I am. (This is an excellent time to pause and listen to what else God wants to give you. Write these down to meditate on later.)

You can do identificational repentance on behalf of any group you are a part of or identify with. It's not only your family. In all cases, you are not saying you have taken part in whatever it is you're repenting of. Instead, you can stand in the gap for the group at large because you are a part of the group. You can think in terms of culture, race, denomination, role in society, gender, position, occupation, etc. For example, I've done identificational repentance for clients on behalf of church leadership even though I wasn't a part of the church that hurt my client but because I have held positions of leadership within the church. You can use this powerful tool to set others free.

Generational Blessings

Generational issues not only pressure you to sin but also block the rightful inheritance the Lord has for your bloodline. Not only do I want you to be free from the enemy's torment, but I also want you to be released into all the Lord has for you.

You may or may not know what your inheritance should have been. In either case, ask the Lord to reveal what the inheritance is to you and how you can access it. My book with Del Hungerford and Seneca Schurbon *Accessing Your Spiritual Inheritance,* covers this in much more depth than I can here. In short, ask God for dreams and visions and then ask him to go with you into those areas and follow his lead on what to do. This might be easier to do after you've completed all the steps in this book. So if you're struggling to understand inheritance, then make a note to return to this after you've finished the book.

Forgiveness

FORGIVENESS IS ONE of the major blockages to healing of all kinds. Holding unforgiveness toward yourself or others gives the enemy permission to torment you. You might have heard that unforgiveness is like drinking poison and expecting the other person to die.[11] It doesn't work. It also allows that person to live rent-free in your head.[12] Not a good idea!

Forgiveness is a process, however, and the larger the issue being forgiven, often the longer the process. The process, however begins with your willingness to forgive the person, God, or even yourself. Once you decide to forgive, remind yourself that you've decided to forgive, and move on again when those ugly feelings come back up,.

The process of forgiveness often depends on the degree of hurt that someone caused. The process can be lengthy, but doing the work is well worth it so that you are completely set free from whatever they did to hurt you. The decision to forgive is a one-time event; the process of forgiving can take years. It becomes easier the more you remind yourself of your decision to forgive, but you might have many layers to work through, depending on the effects these actions had in your life. Give yourself grace for this journey. It is well worth it!

---

11 Emmet Fox, The Sermon on the Mount (Houston: Harper & Brothers, 1938), 99.
12 Esther Lederer (Ann Landers), Wildmind Meditation, October 31. 2007, accessed April 27, 2019, https://www.wildmind.org/blogs/quote-of-the-month/ann-landers-resentment.

Often, the person we struggle the most to forgive is our self. Holding a grudge against yourself really does you no favors, however. Jesus forgives you freely. Please follow his example and forgive yourself freely as well.

I'm including two sample prayers. Please fill in the blanks as appropriate for you and your situation.

Forgiving Others

I forgive _____ for teaching me that my identity and worth was based on what I do and not who I am. (Repeat as needed and add what you're forgiving them for if needed.) I forgive all who have sinned against me and who have set me up to sin. I forgive all who have hurt me out of their own woundedness. I release them from all I feel they owe me, all judgements I've made against them, and all punishments I wanted them to experience. I replace any curses I've spoken against them with blessings. I release them into your hands, Father, and pray they would find healing from their wounds.

Forgiving Yourself

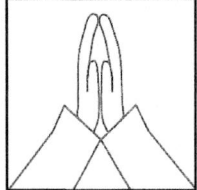

I forgive myself for believing the lies of control because you forgave me. I forgive myself for hurting myself and others out of my woundedness. I release myself from all accusations or judgements and all hatred and slander I made against myself. I forgive myself for making mistakes and falling short of God's best for my life. I accept myself even as you accept me, Jesus, and I ask you to help me learn to love myself as you love me. I trust that, even as I accept myself where I am, you are at work to bring me to greater levels of wholeness and are recreating me into your image. I give myself grace for this process of becoming the person you created me to be.

I encourage you to do a Bible study and discover all the blessings that Christ has given you and who he says you are.

Ungodly Beliefs and Lies

G OD WANTS US to believe him and his Word. Our beliefs shape who we are and what we believe about ourselves, others, and God. Ungodly beliefs are contrary to the character of God and his Word. They are typically acquired from painful events you experience, from friends and family, and from your culture. They include lies such as,

- "I have no power unless I control others."
- "I have to be controlled, or I won't accomplish anything"
- "Leaders in my life are there to control me."

Ungodly beliefs shape our experiences and behavior.

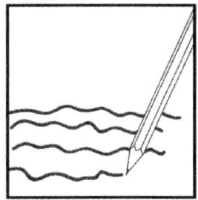

By replacing these ungodly beliefs with godly beliefs, we can reshape our experiences and behavior so that they align with what God says about us. Since ungodly beliefs are such a powerful force in our lives that shape our experiences, they are sometimes difficult for us to find on our own. You can

spot them when you are reading the Bible and you think what you read is not for you. That cynicism alerts you to an ungodly belief. You can also spend time in listening prayer, and ask God to share with you any false beliefs. If you struggle with this or can't spot the lie, seek help from a friend or trusted advisor.

Once you identify an ungodly belief or a lie about control, work your way through the following prayer:

Father, I confess and repent for believing the lie that _____. I forgive any who contributed to the formation of this belief in me, specifically ____ (list whoever comes to mind). I ask you, Father to forgive me for believing this lie and for all the effects this lie has had in my life. Thank you for your forgiveness. Because you forgive me, I can forgive myself for believing this lie and for all the effects it has had in my life. I renounce the belief that _____, and I revoke all agreements made with the enemy related to this belief. I accept the truth that _____. (This is generally the opposite of the lie, but spend quiet time and allow the Lord to speak the truth he wants you to believe.)

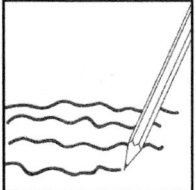

Write out the godly belief and read it aloud several times a day. Also search the Bible for verses reinforcing this new belief and personalize them. Write them out and read them aloud. Continue to do this until the truth saturates your being and shifts your behavior and experiences.

Word Curses

A WORD CURSE IS something negative said to you or about you that you believe and internalize so that it shapes your beliefs about yourself, your abilities, or your circumstances. Typically these also contribute to your failures in some way. You can also speak a word curse about yourself. Some common ones related to control include:

- Others always control me.
- I have to stay in control of others at all times.
- I have to be in control of everything all the time.

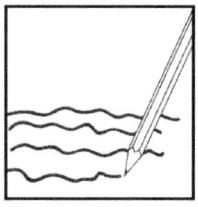

Spend time in prayer and allow the Holy Spirit to reveal any active curses that are impacting you. Once you identify any you have heard or said to yourself, you can break them off with the following prayer.

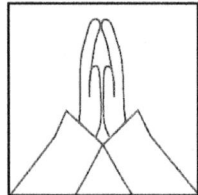

Father, I forgive _____ (this may be yourself), for cursing me by saying _____. (Repeat this for each of the people and curses you've written or what the Holy Spirit reveals to you as you pray.) I repent for believing this curse and for allowing it to shape my beliefs about myself, other people, my circumstances, and you. I ask for and receive your forgiveness. Thank you. I revoke and break all rights these curses had in my life and in my relationships and circumstances. I gather them up and cast them to the cross of Jesus along with any entities involved. I place the blood of Jesus between all that and me. I ask you, Jesus, to help me reverse and correct all the effects of these curses in my life, and help me appropriate the blessings you have for me in place of these curses. Thank you.

Soul Ties

SOUL TIES CAN be godly and healthy or ungodly. While sex is one way a soul tie forms, it is not the only way. We find godly soul ties in close, healthy relationships within healthy boundaries; those are beneficial, and we want to leave them alone or even strengthen them. Ungodly soul ties happen when two people make an inappropriate connection such as, a controlling or manipulative relationship that attempts to take away the free will of the other person. Not only does the ungodly soul tie give the other person more access to you than they should have, it also seems to give the enemy greater access to you.

I recommend praying to break any ungodly soul ties with anyone who comes to mind. If you have no soul ties with that person, then nothing happens, but you do have soul ties with them, then it's best to break them. You might have both godly and ungodly soul ties with the same person, especially your spouse or close family. Therefore, we specify we are breaking the ungodly soul ties.

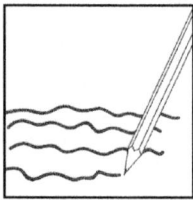

You can ask God for a list of people before you pray or just mention those that come to mind as you pray. You don't need to try to think of anyone and everyone. Just go with whoever immediately comes to mind and then move on. If God reminds you of others later, you can come back and pray again.

Father, I confess and repent of any ungodly soul ties I have with
___. I forgive ___ for their part in creating these soul ties. (Repeat
for each person who comes to mind.) I take back what they have
that is rightfully mine, and I send back to them what I have that
is rightfully theirs, washed in the blood of Jesus and sent with
a message of salvation, healing, and a blessing. I break off these
soul ties. I seal up the connection point with the blood of Jesus.
I revoke any rights the enemy has gained to me through these
soul ties, and I gather up all entities involved and cast them to
the cross of Jesus. I place the blood of Jesus between all that and
me. In Jesus's name. Amen.

Emotional Wounds

ONE OF THE major access points the enemy has to each of us is through unhealed or ineffectively healed emotional wounds. We are hurt many times throughout our lives, but we can handle these hurts in a healthy or unhealthy manner. Sometimes these hurts shape our beliefs about ourselves and others inaccurately. Maybe the person disregarded our feelings, or no one knew how to help us work through what we thought, felt, or experienced. There's probably no end to the various ways people can hurt us. But do we allow God to help us work through those hurts, or do we stuff them, hoping they will go away?

Before we continue, I believe most people do the best they can with what they know: both we who hurt and the ones who are doing the hurting. Most people act in hurtful ways because of their own woundings. Most people are doing the best they know how given what they've been through. And this is one of the most important reasons for finding healing so that the pattern of hurting others ends with us. We get healed, and we learn how to treat others better, and the world becomes a better place.

In some cases, you might need someone else to help walk you through this process so that you don't become stuck and can keep moving. This depends on how healed you are, how fresh or how deep the wound is, current triggers related to the issue, etc. If you become stuck, this is a perfect time to phone a

friend, or seek a minister who can help you navigate this process. There is no shame in seeking help. The point is to get healed!

I recommend you take one memory or hurt at a time and go through the process. If more than one occasion of the same hurt comes to mind, you can often deal with them as a group. Just set your intention to include each incident that hurt occurred in your life. If you have different incidents, make a note of the others, and pick one to start with. You can keep going through your list until they are all done although you might need to take time for your system to recover after each of them. Again, this depends on how the hurts affected you.

The following is a basic template I use during sessions with clients. It is a guide, not a super rigid framework. This order is generally best because I've found it to be the most effective. But sometimes you need to go back to an earlier point and then move forward.

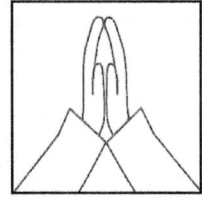

1. Ask Jesus or the Holy Spirit to take you to the first memory of hurt related to control.
2. Tell Jesus how you are feeling in that memory.
3. Give all those negative emotions to Jesus. Some people find it helpful to picture pulling the negativity out of each cell or body part, starting at the toes and working upward, finally giving it all to Jesus or placing it at the foot of the cross. Sometimes you need to take each emotion, one at a time, and give it to Jesus. Other times, you can gather up the whole mess at once and give it to him. Keep doing this until you've given it all to him or placed it all at the cross.
4. Place the blood of Jesus between all the negativity and you. Ask Jesus to fill you with the opposite of what you've just released, e.g., his patience, love, hope, belonging, etc.

5. Invite Jesus into the memory to heal your hurt. Watch and wait to see what he does. He might want to take you to the Father.
6. You might need to revisit some earlier chapters and walk through forgiveness, ungodly lies and beliefs, etc.

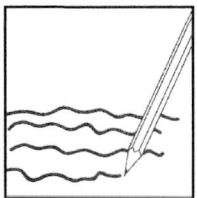

7. When you've finished all the healing, ask Jesus, Father, or the Holy Spirit to tell you what he thinks of you or of the situation as appropriate. Write what you see, hear, feel, or sense.

You can repeat this process for all hurts related to control or any other issue you're dealing with. This is also effective for current hurts.

Demonic Oppression

I 'VE OFTEN HEARD the demonic described as rats feeding on garbage. Part of what we've been doing so far in this book is getting rid of the garbage of control so that the rats have nothing left to attach to or feed on. Little by little, we've eliminated the contact points or rights we've given the enemy. Once we heal, break, and close off their rights, access, and contact points, we can easily kick them off.

We usually name the demonic by their function. Since we've been dealing with control, we will get rid of the demons of control and any under their authority or involved with them. Sometimes you can just toss the whole package, and sometimes you need to specifically name them one by one. Just repeat the prayer as often as you need to until you've eliminated them all. If you think of others later, just pray through the prayer again.

You'll notice this is not a complicated prayer. It's simple but powerful. Through Christ, you have authority over the enemy, especially when you've removed any rights the enemy has to be there. This is a legal proceeding not a power play, so volume is unnecessary. The enemy is not hearing-impaired, and he knows better than we do the authority we carry. So he often relies on hiddenness, darkness, and intimidation. But we've seen his plan and foiled his plots, so let's kick him out!

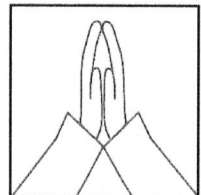

1. Father, forgive me for buying into the lies of control, for giving control access to my life through all the generational issues, soul ties, unforgiveness, ungodly beliefs, word curses, and woundings.
2. I forgive myself for buying into the lies of control, and I accept your forgiveness.
3. I renounce, break, and cancel all agreements made with control along with any other entity under its authority or affiliated with it. (Name any that come to mind, but don't linger here.)
4. I gather up control and all entities involved in any way (including the list in #3 as needed) and cast them to the cross of Jesus. I place the blood of Jesus between all that and me.
5. I ask you, Jesus, to fill me with your peace and wholeness (and the opposite of the entities you've mentioned). Please teach me how to walk in your ___ as I move forward in my life.

Overcoming Triggers

Triggers

T RIGGERS SET OFF an undesired reaction or initiate poor behavioral choices, such as stress eating or retail therapy. Triggers can make you feel as if you are back in a traumatic or very stressful situation even though you are miles or years away from it. A trigger can also be overreacting to a particular situation because you're not only reacting to the present but to the past as well.

Possible Roots

Triggers can result from any traumatic situation in your past. Science is discovering, through epigenetics, that you might not only be reacting to your past. You could be reacting to that of your ancestors as well.

I often describe triggers like a bruise. Normally when you poke your arm, it doesn't hurt much. But if you have a bruise and poke it, it hurts a lot. Triggers are the poke; what gets triggered is the bruise. Unhealed trauma unfortunately doesn't just go away. It stays with us and helps to shape our reactions and responses to new situations.

Sometimes people describe themselves as "acting or feeling as if I'm five" or some other childhood age. That's likely because the original wound happened when they were five, and so when something similar happens all these years later, they are still reacting from that place of a hurt five-year-old. Those wounded places within us are very powerful, but there is hope! You can get free, and it's a beautiful thing when you successfully deal with a trigger. In other words, something happened that once would have triggered you, but now it doesn't because you've received such deep healing!

We'll be dealing with triggers in a general way, but you may need to work through whatever trauma is at the root of those triggers in a more detailed way. See any of the rest of the books in this series as needed.

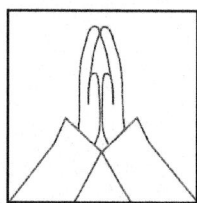

Father, I come before you this day because I need your help to access the freedom from triggers. Jesus purchased for me on the cross. I take authority over myself, my space, and my will, and I submit myself to you and agree with you completely wherever you lead me through this process. I remove anything within myself that's hiding this issue and cut off all enemy access, placing everything into Jesus's hands. I ask you, Lord Jesus, to gather up and bind all warfare that would seek to hinder me from becoming free from triggers or any other issue. Please send the angelic support I need.

I repent of all enemy rights and agreements and suspend them from all areas of access he has. I place them into Jesus's hands to keep during my work. Thank you, Father, for your provision and protection.

I ask you, Holy Spirit, for any blessings I need as I do this work. I ask for an anointing of power and authority as I address this issue. Please give me clarity of thought and intention and a breakthrough in healing. In Jesus's name. Amen.

Generational Issues

APART OF MANY inner healing protocols and methods is a process that goes by different names. I use the phrase "generational work", but I've heard the terms ancestral cleansing and bloodline clearing, among others. As far as I know, these teachings are all based on the idea that the sins of our fathers (and mothers) can negatively impact us today.

You can see this most clearly when there is a strong family history of abuse or alcoholism. In fact, one scientific study shows that family members of alcoholics run three times the risk of alcohol abuse while for family members of other substance abusers, the risk is twice as high when compared with those who have no family history of alcohol abuse.[13]

Generational issues also manifest in a family history of poverty, anger, sexual, or even health issues. The theory is that when an ancestor started down that path, for whatever reason, their children, grandchildren, etc., carried on this destructive tradition. These issues might even be more subtle than the listed examples. For instance, overcoming an issue is much more difficult than it should be, and it's a constant battle to stay free. Maybe the people in

---

13 K. C. Pears, D. M. Capaldi, and L. D. Owen "Substance Use Risk Across Three Generations: The Roles of Parent Discipline Practices and Inhibitory Control," US National Library of Medicine National Institutes of Health, September 21, 2007, 21(3): 373–386. https://www.ncbi.nlm.nih.gov/pmc/articles/PMC1988842.

your bloodline are overweight, but you are not. But you struggle to maintain a healthy weight, for example.

I don't believe that all our sins are generational or affect the generations after us. But some clearly seem to. And the enemy is often at work in the middle of the mess. He is ever watching to catch us at our weakest. His job description is to steal, kill, and destroy, and he doesn't seem to ever go on vacation. (See John 10:10.)

Before I go any further, I want to emphasize that you are not held personally responsible for your ancestor's sin. You are only responsible for your own sins. But the generational piece adds a pressure or weight that increases the likelihood that you might sin in a particular area. We have a choice whether or not we enter into the sin, but even if we don't, the generational piece seems to make the fight against that sin more difficult than it needs to be.

The Process

1. What Are We Dealing with?

Pray and ask God to show you where the trigger started or what the initial wound was. Once you know the starting point, then it's easy. The enemy operates best in hiddenness and darkness. Once we know what we're dealing with, he doesn't stand much of a chance. Note: If you are adopted, then you have two sets of parents to potentially deal with. Since adoption is a physical and legal transaction, this seems to impact the spiritual realm as well.

2. Confession and Repentance

Identificational repentance clears the enemy's access to us because of generational issues. This means repenting on behalf of a larger group you're part of, in this case, your family. Again, you are not necessarily saying you are guilty of those sins, but you are standing in the gap for your family to remove the access the enemy has on you and your bloodline.

Nehemiah shows us this when he asked God to forgive "us" for the state of the walls of Jerusalem. He had nothing to do with the broken-down walls. You aren't saying you are guilty of the sin; you are saying you are sorry it happened and that the enemy has gained access to your bloodline because of it.

You then want to repent on your ancestor's behalf for committing this sin and allowing it access to your bloodline. (You do not need specific details about the sin.) Forgive them where appropriate. Then confess and repent on behalf of each generation from that time until now for not addressing this matter or for allowing it access. Also confess and repent of any way you have come into agreement with this sin, which removes the enemy's legal rights to our bloodline. We've already weakened its hold by releasing the negative emotions.

3. Eliminate the Warfare

Now that you have ended the enemy's rights, gather them up and cast them to the cross of Jesus. Revoke all rights to you and your bloodline and place the blood of Jesus between all that mess and all of your bloodline. Remember, you are doing this on behalf of all the descendants of that original person. I don't know how far out that reaches, but I am personally aware distant family members set free from migraines because one person addressed these issues. You have more influence than you think!

4. Input the Positive

We then release the opposite spirit of the demonic attack and all the good things of God that pertain to your life and to the lives of your family members and all those impacted by this generational issue. I pray from a logical standpoint. For instance, if with the issue relates to anger, I release love and peace, etc., but I also listen for the Spirit to lead. We want you and your bloodline to be full of the things of God.

We cannot control the choices that others make. You are not responsible for anyone's choices and behaviors but your own. But when you are under the weight of a generational piece, you don't know that you have another

choice. The removal of this dark cloud over your bloodline opens realms of possibilities to choose a better path. Breaking this generational issue doesn't mean that you never engage in the former behavior or thought process again although that can happen. But sometimes we need to walk out the matter and practice making better choices. Once you are free from the generational issue, it should be much easier than it was before.

The following is a sample prayer to walk through step-by-step, but this is also the perfect time to practice listening prayer. Only the Holy Spirit knows the full effects of this generational issue on your life, so listen carefully to his voice as you walk through this process and pray additional points as he leads you. Read through the prayer first and then make a note of anything the Holy Spirit wants you to add before you begin. You can also stop after each point, make notes, and then pray as you go.

I'm going to leave blanks here. Insert the sin of the initial wounding—either what you did or what was done to you. It can be a general category such as anger, shame, abuse, etc.

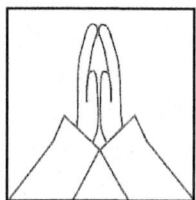

1. I confess that my ancestors came into agreement with _____, believing that what we do is our identity. Through this, they allowed the enemy access to their bloodline. I repent on each person's behalf for committing this sin and allowing the enemy access to us. I forgive them. I also confess and repent on behalf of myself and every other member of my bloodline who came into agreement with _____, including associated sins or agreements of _____.

2. I forgive myself and all those in my bloodline who have committed the sin of _____ or who have influenced me to take part in this sin and for the consequences of that sin in my life. (Specifically name anyone the Holy Spirit brings to your mind.)

3. I ask you to forgive me, Jesus, for agreeing with this issue and for committing these sins. I receive your forgiveness, and I forgive myself for taking part in this issue and for all the effects it has had on my life.

4. I revoke all agreements with _____ on my behalf and as much as I can on behalf of all those in my bloodline. I revoke any agreements I or my family made with the entities of _____ or any others affiliated with this or under their authority. I revoke all their rights to me and my entire bloodline past, present, and future from this time forward.

5. I gather up all these entities and agreements, and I cast them to the cross of Jesus. I place the blood of Jesus between all that and myself and my entire bloodline. I reverse and correct all the effects of _____ in my life and in the lives of my family.

6. On behalf of my family, I receive the freedom Jesus Christ bought for me when he died on the cross and rose again, defeating all the works of the enemy. I receive his identity and courage and choose to listen to what he says about who I am. (This is an excellent time to pause and listen to what else God wants to give you. Write these down to meditate on later.)

You can do identificational repentance on behalf of any group you are a part of or identify with. It's not only your family. In all cases, you are not saying you have taken part in whatever it is you're repenting of. Instead, you can stand in the gap for the group at large because you are a part of the group. You can think in terms of culture, race, denomination, role in society, gender, position, occupation, etc. For example, I've done identificational repentance for clients on behalf of church leadership even though I wasn't a part of the church that hurt my client but because I have held positions of leadership within the church. You can use this powerful tool to set others free.

Generational Blessings

Generational issues not only pressure you to sin but also block the rightful inheritance the Lord has for your bloodline. Not only do I want you to be

free from the enemy's torment, but I also want you to be released into all the Lord has for you.

You may or may not know what your inheritance should have been. In either case, ask the Lord to reveal what the inheritance is to you and how you can access it. My book with Del Hungerford and Seneca Schurbon *Accessing Your Spiritual Inheritance,* covers this in much more depth than I can here. In short, ask God for dreams and visions and then ask him to go with you into those areas and follow his lead on what to do. This might be easier to do after you've completed all the steps in this book. So if you're struggling to understand inheritance, then make a note to return to this after you've finished the book.

Forgiveness

ORGIVENESS IS ONE of the major blockages to healing of all kinds. Holding unforgiveness toward yourself or others gives the enemy permission to torment you. You might have heard that unforgiveness is like drinking poison and expecting the other person to die.[14] It doesn't work. It also allows that person to live rent-free in your head.[15] Not a good idea!

Forgiveness is a process, however, and the larger the issue being forgiven, often the longer the process. The process, however begins with your willingness to forgive the person, God, or even yourself. Once you decide to forgive, remind yourself that you've decided to forgive, and move on again when those ugly feelings come back up,.

The process of forgiveness often depends on the degree of hurt that someone caused. The process can be lengthy, but doing the work is well worth it so that you are completely set free from whatever they did to hurt you. The decision to forgive is a one-time event; the process of forgiving can take years. It becomes easier the more you remind yourself of your decision to forgive, but you might have many layers to work through, depending on the effects these actions had in your life. Give yourself grace for this journey. It is well worth it!

---

14 Emmet Fox, The Sermon on the Mount (Houston: Harper & Brothers, 1938), 99.
15 Esther Lederer (Ann Landers), Wildmind Meditation, October 31. 2007, accessed April 27, 2019, https://www.wildmind.org/blogs/quote-of-the-month/ann-landers-resentment.

Often, the person we struggle the most to forgive is our self. Holding a grudge against yourself really does you no favors, however. Jesus forgives you freely. Please follow his example and forgive yourself freely as well.

I'm including two sample prayers. Please fill in the blanks as appropriate for you and your situation.

Forgiving Others

I forgive _____ for teaching me that my identity and worth was based on what I do and not who I am. (Repeat as needed and add what you're forgiving them for if needed.) I forgive all who have sinned against me and who have set me up to sin. I forgive all who have hurt me out of their own woundedness. I release them from all I feel they owe me, all judgements I've made against them, and all punishments I wanted them to experience. I replace any curses I've spoken against them with blessings. I release them into your hands, Father, and pray they would find healing from their wounds.

Forgiving Yourself

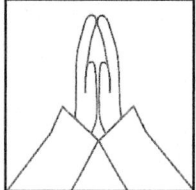

I forgive myself for getting triggered or experiencing the initial trauma because you forgave me. I forgive myself for hurting myself and others out of my woundedness. I release myself from all accusations or judgements and all hatred and slander I made against myself. I forgive myself for making mistakes and falling short of God's best for my life. I accept myself even as you accept me, Jesus, and I ask you to help me learn to love myself as you love me. I trust that, even as I accept myself where I am, you are at work to bring me to greater levels of wholeness and are recreating me into your image. I give myself grace for this process of becoming the person you created me to be.

I encourage you to do a Bible study and discover all the blessings that Christ has given you and who he says you are.

Ungodly Beliefs and Lies

GOD WANTS US to believe him and his Word. Our beliefs shape who we are and what we believe about ourselves, others, and God. Ungodly beliefs are contrary to the character of God and his Word. They are typically acquired from painful events you experience, from friends and family, and from your culture. They include lies such as,

- "I have no ability to heal from this."
- "I will always be triggered by this."
- "There is no hope for this; it's just the way I am."

Ungodly beliefs shape our experiences and behavior.

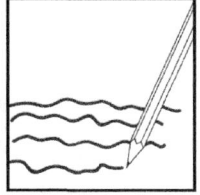

By replacing these ungodly beliefs with godly beliefs, we can reshape our experiences and behavior so that they align with what God says about us. Since ungodly beliefs are such a powerful force in our lives that shape our experiences, they are sometimes difficult for us to find on our own. You can

spot them when you are reading the Bible and you think what you read is not for you. That cynicism alerts you to an ungodly belief. You can also spend time in listening prayer, and ask God to share with you any false beliefs. If you struggle with this or can't spot the lie, seek help from a friend or trusted advisor.

Once you identify an ungodly belief or a lie about triggers, work your way through the following prayer:

Father, I confess and repent for believing the lie that _____. I forgive any who contributed to the formation of this belief in me, specifically ____ (list whoever comes to mind). I ask you, Father to forgive me for believing this lie and for all the effects this lie has had in my life. Thank you for your forgiveness. Because you forgive me, I can forgive myself for believing this lie and for all the effects it has had in my life. I renounce the belief that _____, and I revoke all agreements made with the enemy related to this belief. I accept the truth that _____. (This is generally the opposite of the lie, but spend quiet time and allow the Lord to speak the truth he wants you to believe.)

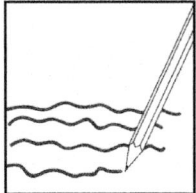

Write out the godly belief and read it aloud several times a day. Also search the Bible for verses reinforcing this new belief and personalize them. Write them out and read them aloud. Continue to do this until the truth saturates your being and shifts your behavior and experiences.

Word Curses

A WORD CURSE IS something negative said to you or about you that you believe and internalize so that it shapes your beliefs about yourself, your abilities, or your circumstances. Typically these also contribute to your failures in some way. You can also speak a word curse about yourself. Some common ones related to triggers include:

- I'm always triggered by _____.
- I can never forgive them; it still hurts too much.
- I'll always be damaged by _____.
- I can never lead a normal life because _____.

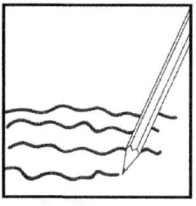

Spend time in prayer and allow the Holy Spirit to reveal any active curses that are impacting you. Once you identify any you have heard or said to yourself, you can break them off with the following prayer.

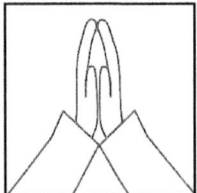

Father, I forgive _____ (this may be yourself), for cursing me by saying _____. (Repeat this for each of the people and curses you've written or what the Holy Spirit reveals to you as you pray.) I repent for believing this curse and for allowing it to shape my beliefs about myself, other people, my circumstances, and you. I ask for and receive your forgiveness. Thank you. I revoke and break all rights these curses had in my life and in my relationships and circumstances. I gather them up and cast them to the cross of Jesus along with any entities involved. I place the blood of Jesus between all that and me. I ask you, Jesus, to help me reverse and correct all the effects of these curses in my life, and help me appropriate the blessings you have for me in place of these curses. Thank you.

Soul Ties

SOUL TIES CAN be godly and healthy or ungodly. While sex is one way a soul tie forms, it is not the only way. We find godly soul ties in close, healthy relationships within healthy boundaries; those are beneficial, and we want to leave them alone or even strengthen them. Ungodly soul ties happen when two people make an inappropriate connection such as, a controlling or manipulative relationship that attempts to take away the free will of the other person. Not only does the ungodly soul tie give the other person more access to you than they should have, it also seems to give the enemy greater access to you.

I recommend praying to break any ungodly soul ties with anyone who comes to mind. If you have no soul ties with that person, then nothing happens, but you do have soul ties with them, then it's best to break them. You might have both godly and ungodly soul ties with the same person, especially your spouse or close family. Therefore, we specify we are breaking the ungodly soul ties.

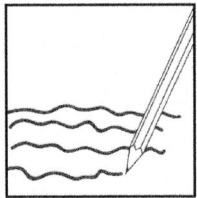

You can ask God for a list of people before you pray or just mention those that come to mind as you pray. You don't need to try to think of anyone and everyone. Just go with whoever immediately comes to mind and then move on. If God reminds you of others later, you can come back and pray again.

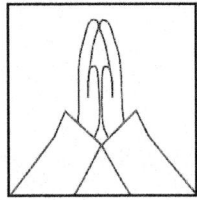

Father, I confess and repent of any ungodly soul ties I have with ___. I forgive ___ for their part in creating these soul ties. (Repeat for each person who comes to mind.) I take back what they have that is rightfully mine, and I send back to them what I have that is rightfully theirs, washed in the blood of Jesus and sent with a message of salvation, healing, and a blessing. I break off these soul ties. I seal up the connection point with the blood of Jesus. I revoke any rights the enemy has gained to me through these soul ties, and I gather up all entities involved and cast them to the cross of Jesus. I place the blood of Jesus between all that and me. In Jesus's name. Amen.

Emotional Wounds

ONE OF THE major access points the enemy has to each of us is through unhealed or ineffectively healed emotional wounds. We are hurt many times throughout our lives, but we can handle these hurts in a healthy or unhealthy manner. Sometimes these hurts shape our beliefs about ourselves and others inaccurately. Maybe the person disregarded our feelings, or no one knew how to help us work through what we thought, felt, or experienced. There's probably no end to the various ways people can hurt us. But do we allow God to help us work through those hurts, or do we stuff them, hoping they will go away?

Before we continue, I believe most people do the best they can with what they know: both we who hurt and the ones who are doing the hurting. Most people act in hurtful ways because of their own woundings. Most people are doing the best they know how given what they've been through. And this is one of the most important reasons for finding healing so that the pattern of hurting others ends with us. We get healed, and we learn how to treat others better, and the world becomes a better place.

In some cases, you might need someone else to help walk you through this process so that you don't become stuck and can keep moving. This depends on how healed you are, how fresh or how deep the wound is, current triggers related to the issue, etc. If you become stuck, this is a perfect time to phone a

friend, or seek a minister who can help you navigate this process. There is no shame in seeking help. The point is to get healed!

I recommend you take one memory or hurt at a time and go through the process. If more than one occasion of the same hurt comes to mind, you can often deal with them as a group. Just set your intention to include each incident that hurt occurred in your life. If you have different incidents, make a note of the others, and pick one to start with. You can keep going through your list until they are all done although you might need to take time for your system to recover after each of them. Again, this depends on how the hurts affected you.

The following is a basic template I use during sessions with clients. It is a guide, not a super rigid framework. This order is generally best because I've found it to be the most effective. But sometimes you need to go back to an earlier point and then move forward.

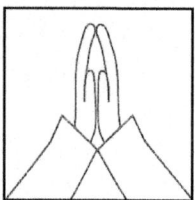

1. Ask Jesus or the Holy Spirit to take you to the first memory of hurt related to the trigger.
2. Tell Jesus how you are feeling in that memory.
3. Give all those negative emotions to Jesus. Some people find it helpful to picture pulling the negativity out of each cell or body part, starting at the toes and working upward, finally giving it all to Jesus or placing it at the foot of the cross. Sometimes you need to take each emotion, one at a time, and give it to Jesus. Other times, you can gather up the whole mess at once and give it to him. Keep doing this until you've given it all to him or placed it all at the cross.
4. Place the blood of Jesus between all the negativity and you. Ask Jesus to fill you with the opposite of what you've just released, e.g., his patience, love, hope, belonging, etc.

5. Invite Jesus into the memory to heal your hurt. Watch and wait to see what he does. He might want to take you to the Father.

6. You might need to revisit some earlier chapters and walk through forgiveness, ungodly lies and beliefs, etc.

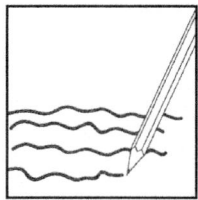

7. When you've finished all the healing, ask Jesus, Father, or the Holy Spirit to tell you what he thinks of you or of the situation as appropriate. Write what you see, hear, feel, or sense.

You can repeat this process for all hurts related to the trigger or any other issue you're dealing with. This is also effective for current hurts.

Demonic Oppression

I'VE OFTEN HEARD the demonic described as rats feeding on garbage. Part of what we've been doing so far in this book is getting rid of the garbage of the triggers so that the rats have nothing left to attach to or feed on. Little by little, we've eliminated the contact points or rights we've given the enemy. Once we heal, break, and close off their rights, access, and contact points, we can easily kick them off.

Again, I'm going to leave blanks here. Insert the sin of the initial wounding—either what you did or what was done to you. It can be a general category such as anger, shame, abuse, etc.

We usually name the demonic by their function. Since we've been dealing with _____, we will get rid of the demons of _____ and any under their authority or involved with them. Sometimes you can just toss the whole package, and sometimes you need to specifically name them one by one. Just repeat the prayer as often as you need to until you've eliminated them all. If you think of others later, just pray through the prayer again.

You'll notice this is not a complicated prayer. It's simple but powerful. Through Christ, you have authority over the enemy, especially when you've removed any rights the enemy has to be there. This is a legal proceeding not a power play, so volume is unnecessary. The enemy is not hearing-impaired, and he knows better than we do the authority we carry. So he often relies on hiddenness, darkness, and intimidation. But we've seen his plan and foiled his plots, so let's kick him out!

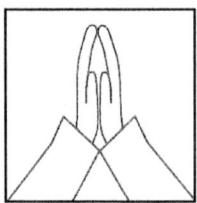

1. Father, forgive me for buying into the lies of _____, for giving _____ access to my life through all the generational issues, soul ties, unforgiveness, ungodly beliefs, word curses, and woundings.

2. I forgive myself for buying into the lies of _____, and I accept your forgiveness.

3. I renounce, break, and cancel all agreements made with _____ along with any other entity under its authority or affiliated with it. (Name any that come to mind, but don't linger here.)

4. I gather up _____ and all entities involved in any way (including the list in #3 as needed) and cast them to the cross of Jesus. I place the blood of Jesus between all that and me.

5. I ask you, Jesus, to fill me with your peace and wholeness (and the opposite of the entities you've mentioned). Please teach me how to walk in your ___ as I move forward in my life.

Overcoming Jealousy

Jealousy

J EALOUSY. IT'S WHEN you can't stand it when others are blessed or do fun activities or have what you don't have or, at least, appear to have what you want. Or jealousy might mean being afraid that someone will take what you have. You might try and belittle or demean others and what they do or have so that you feel better in comparison.

In its more subtle forms, it can sound like: "I wish I could sing as well as Suzy." "I wish I could find a man like Fred." "She/He has it so easy. Why can't life be easy for me?"

Possible Roots

Jealousy is rooted in insecurity and a lack of knowledge or understanding of who we are uniquely created, gifted, and called to be. It's all about comparing who we are or want to be with those around us.

It also has roots in a poverty or limited mindset. Jealousy says that there's not enough to go around, so I have to fight for what I think I should have. And if I can't have it, they can't either.

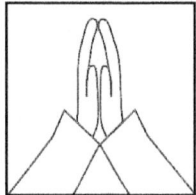

Father, I come before you this day because I need your help to access the freedom from jealousy. Jesus purchased for me on the cross. I take authority over myself, my space, and my will, and I submit myself to you and agree with you completely wherever you lead me through this process. I remove anything within myself that's hiding this issue and cut off all enemy access, placing everything into Jesus's hands. I ask you, Lord Jesus, to gather up and bind all warfare that would seek to hinder me from becoming free from jealousy or any other issue. Please send the angelic support I need.

I repent of all enemy rights and agreements and suspend them from all areas of access he has. I place them into Jesus's hands to keep during my work. Thank you, Father, for your provision and protection.

I ask you, Holy Spirit, for any blessings I need as I do this work. I ask for an anointing of power and authority as I address this issue. Please give me clarity of thought and intention and a breakthrough in healing. In Jesus's name. Amen.

Generational Issues

APART OF MANY inner healing protocols and methods is a process that goes by different names. I use the phrase "generational work," but I've heard the terms ancestral cleansing and bloodline clearing, among others. As far as I know, these teachings are all based on the idea that the sins of our fathers (and mothers) can negatively impact us today.

You can see this most clearly when there is a strong family history of abuse or alcoholism. In fact, one scientific study shows that family members of alcoholics run three times the risk of alcohol abuse while for family members of other substance abusers, the risk is twice as high when compared with those who have no family history of alcohol abuse.[16]

Generational issues also manifest in a family history of poverty, anger, sexual, or even health issues. The theory is that when an ancestor started down that path, for whatever reason, their children, grandchildren, etc., carried on this destructive tradition. These issues might even be more subtle than the listed examples. For instance, overcoming an issue is much more difficult than it should be, and it's a constant battle to stay free. Maybe the people in

---

16 K. C. Pears, D. M. Capaldi, and L. D. Owen "Substance Use Risk Across Three Generations: The Roles of Parent Discipline Practices and Inhibitory Control," US National Library of Medicine National Institutes of Health, September 21, 2007, 21(3): 373–386. https://www.ncbi.nlm.nih.gov/pmc/articles/PMC1988842.

your bloodline are overweight, but you are not. But you struggle to maintain a healthy weight, for example.

I don't believe that all our sins are generational or affect the generations after us. But some clearly seem to. And the enemy is often at work in the middle of the mess. He is ever watching to catch us at our weakest. His job description is to steal, kill, and destroy, and he doesn't seem to ever go on vacation. (See John 10:10.)

Before I go any further, I want to emphasize that you are not held personally responsible for your ancestor's sin. You are only responsible for your own sins. But the generational piece adds a pressure or weight that increases the likelihood that you might sin in a particular area. We have a choice whether or not we enter into the sin, but even if we don't, the generational piece seems to make the fight against that sin more difficult than it needs to be.

The Process

1. What Are We Dealing with?

Pray and ask God to show you where the jealousy started. Once you know the starting point, then it's easy. The enemy operates best in hiddenness and darkness. Once we know what we're dealing with, he doesn't stand much of a chance. Note: If you are adopted, then you have two sets of parents to potentially deal with. Since adoption is a physical and legal transaction, this seems to impact the spiritual realm as well.

2. Confession and Repentance

Identificational repentance clears the enemy's access to us because of generational issues. This means repenting on behalf of a larger group you're part of, in this case, your family. Again, you are not necessarily saying you are guilty of those sins, but you are standing in the gap for your family to remove the access the enemy has on you and your bloodline.

Nehemiah shows us this when he asked God to forgive "us" for the state of the walls of Jerusalem. He had nothing to do with the broken-down walls. You aren't saying you are guilty of the sin; you are saying you are sorry it happened and that the enemy has gained access to your bloodline because of it.

You then want to repent on your ancestor's behalf for committing this sin and allowing it access to your bloodline. (You do not need specific details about the sin.) Forgive them where appropriate. Then confess and repent on behalf of each generation from that time until now for not addressing this matter or for allowing it access. Also confess and repent of any way you have come into agreement with this sin, which removes the enemy's legal rights to our bloodline. We've already weakened its hold by releasing the negative emotions.

3. Eliminate the Warfare

Now that you have ended the enemy's rights, gather them up and cast them to the cross of Jesus. Revoke all rights to you and your bloodline and place the blood of Jesus between all that mess and all of your bloodline. Remember, you are doing this on behalf of all the descendants of that original person. I don't know how far out that reaches, but I am personally aware distant family members set free from migraines because one person addressed these issues. You have more influence than you think!

4. Input the Positive

We then release the opposite spirit of the demonic attack and all the good things of God that pertain to your life and to the lives of your family members and all those impacted by this generational issue. I pray from a logical standpoint. For instance, if with the issue relates to anger, I release love and peace, etc., but I also listen for the Spirit to lead. We want you and your bloodline to be full of the things of God.

We cannot control the choices that others make. You are not responsible for anyone's choices and behaviors but your own. But when you are under the weight of a generational piece, you don't know that you have another choice. The removal of this dark cloud over your bloodline opens realms of possibilities to choose a better path. Breaking this generational issue doesn't mean that you never engage in the former behavior or thought process again although that can happen. But sometimes we need to walk out the matter and practice making better choices. Once you are free from the generational issue, it should be much easier than it was before.

The following is a sample prayer to walk through step-by-step, but this is also the perfect time to practice listening prayer. Only the Holy Spirit knows the full effects of this generational issue on your life, so listen carefully to his voice as you walk through this process and pray additional points as he leads you. Read through the prayer first and then make a note of anything the Holy Spirit wants you to add before you begin. You can also stop after each point, make notes, and then pray as you go.

I'm going to leave blanks here. Insert the sin of the initial wounding— either what you did or what was done to you. It can be a general category such as anger, shame, abuse, etc.

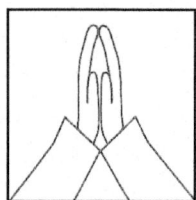

1. I confess that my ancestors came into agreement with jealousy, believing that what we do is our identity. Through this, they allowed the enemy access to their bloodline. I repent on each person's behalf for committing this sin and allowing the enemy access to us. I forgive them. I also confess and repent on behalf of myself and every other member of my bloodline who came into agreement with jealousy, including associated sins or agreements of insecurity, poverty mindset, etc.

2. I forgive myself and all those in my bloodline who have committed the sin of jealousy or who have influenced me to take part in this sin and for the consequences of that sin in my life. (Specifically name anyone the Holy Spirit brings to your mind.)

3. I ask you to forgive me, Jesus, for agreeing with this issue and for committing these sins. I receive your forgiveness, and I forgive myself for taking part in this issue and for all the effects it has had on my life.

4. I revoke all agreements with jealousy on my behalf and as much as I can on behalf of all those in my bloodline. I revoke any agreements I or my family made with the entities of jealousy or any others affiliated with this or under their authority. I revoke all their rights to me and my entire bloodline past, present, and future from this time forward.

5. I gather up all these entities and agreements, and I cast them to the cross of Jesus. I place the blood of Jesus between all that and myself and my entire bloodline. I reverse and correct all the effects of jealousy in my life and in the lives of my family.

6. On behalf of my family, I receive the freedom Jesus Christ bought for me when he died on the cross and rose again, defeating all the works of the enemy. I receive his identity and courage and choose to listen to what he says about who I am. (This is an excellent time to pause and listen to what else God wants to give you. Write these down to meditate on later.)

You can do identificational repentance on behalf of any group you are a part of or identify with. It's not only your family. In all cases, you are not saying you have taken part in whatever it is you're repenting of. Instead, you can stand in the gap for the group at large because you are a part of the group. You can think in terms of culture, race, denomination, role in society, gender, position, occupation, etc. For example, I've done identificational repentance for clients on behalf of church leadership even though I wasn't a part of the church that hurt my client but because I have held positions of leadership within the church. You can use this powerful tool to set others free.

Generational Blessings

Generational issues not only pressure you to sin but also block the rightful inheritance the Lord has for your bloodline. Not only do I want you to be

free from the enemy's torment, but I also want you to be released into all the Lord has for you.

You may or may not know what your inheritance should have been. In either case, ask the Lord to reveal what the inheritance is to you and how you can access it. My book with Del Hungerford and Seneca Schurbon *Accessing Your Spiritual Inheritance,* covers this in much more depth than I can here. In short, ask God for dreams and visions and then ask him to go with you into those areas and follow his lead on what to do. This might be easier to do after you've completed all the steps in this book. So if you're struggling to understand inheritance, then make a note to return to this after you've finished the book.

Forgiveness

F ORGIVENESS IS ONE of the major blockages to healing of all kinds. Holding unforgiveness toward yourself or others gives the enemy permission to torment you. You might have heard that unforgiveness is like drinking poison and expecting the other person to die.[17] It doesn't work. It also allows that person to live rent-free in your head.[18] Not a good idea!

Forgiveness is a process, however, and the larger the issue being forgiven, often the longer the process. The process, however begins with your willingness to forgive the person, God, or even yourself. Once you decide to forgive, remind yourself that you've decided to forgive, and move on again when those ugly feelings come back up,.

The process of forgiveness often depends on the degree of hurt that someone caused. The process can be lengthy, but doing the work is well worth it so that you are completely set free from whatever they did to hurt you. The decision to forgive is a one-time event; the process of forgiving can take years. It becomes easier the more you remind yourself of your decision to forgive, but you might have many layers to work through, depending on the effects these actions had in your life. Give yourself grace for this journey. It is well worth it!

---

17 Emmet Fox, The Sermon on the Mount (Houston: Harper & Brothers, 1938), 99.
18 Esther Lederer (Ann Landers), Wildmind Meditation, October 31. 2007, accessed April 27, 2019, https://www.wildmind.org/blogs/quote-of-the-month/ann-landers-resentment.

Often, the person we struggle the most to forgive is our self. Holding a grudge against yourself really does you no favors, however. Jesus forgives you freely. Please follow his example and forgive yourself freely as well.

I'm including two sample prayers. Please fill in the blanks as appropriate for you and your situation.

Forgiving Others

I forgive _____ for teaching me that my identity and worth was based on what I do and not who I am. (Repeat as needed and add what you're forgiving them for if needed.) I forgive all who have sinned against me and who have set me up to sin. I forgive all who have hurt me out of their own woundedness. I release them from all I feel they owe me, all judgements I've made against them, and all punishments I wanted them to experience. I replace any curses I've spoken against them with blessings. I release them into your hands, Father, and pray they would find healing from their wounds.

Forgiving Yourself

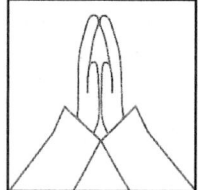

I forgive myself for believing the lies of jealousy because you forgave me. I forgive myself for hurting myself and others out of my woundedness. I release myself from all accusations or judgements and all hatred and slander I made against myself. I forgive myself for making mistakes and falling short of God's best for my life. I accept myself even as you accept me, Jesus, and I ask you to help me learn to love myself as you love me. I trust that, even as I accept myself where I am, you are at work to bring me to greater levels of wholeness and are recreating me into your image. I give myself grace for this process of becoming the person you created me to be.

I encourage you to do a Bible study and discover all the blessings that Christ has given you and who he says you are.

Ungodly Beliefs and Lies

GOD WANTS US to believe him and his Word. Our beliefs shape who we are and what we believe about ourselves, others, and God. Ungodly beliefs are contrary to the character of God and his Word. They are typically acquired from painful events you experience, from friends and family, and from your culture. They include lies such as,

- I deserve _____ more than they do.
- I have to take what I need or else I won't get what's mine.
- I should make myself small so they won't be jealous of me.

Ungodly beliefs shape our experiences and behavior.

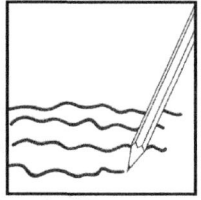

By replacing these ungodly beliefs with godly beliefs, we can reshape our experiences and behavior so that they align with what God says about us. Since ungodly beliefs are such a powerful force in our lives that shape our experiences, they are sometimes difficult for us to find on our own. You can

spot them when you are reading the Bible and you think what you read is not for you. That cynicism alerts you to an ungodly belief. You can also spend time in listening prayer, and ask God to share with you any false beliefs. If you struggle with this or can't spot the lie, seek help from a friend or trusted advisor.

Once you identify an ungodly belief or a lie about jealousy, work your way through the following prayer:

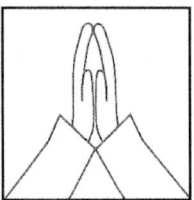

Father, I confess and repent for believing the lie that _____. I forgive any who contributed to the formation of this belief in me, specifically ____ (list whoever comes to mind). I ask you, Father to forgive me for believing this lie and for all the effects this lie has had in my life. Thank you for your forgiveness. Because you forgive me, I can forgive myself for believing this lie and for all the effects it has had in my life. I renounce the belief that _____, and I revoke all agreements made with the enemy related to this belief. I accept the truth that _____. (This is generally the opposite of the lie, but spend quiet time and allow the Lord to speak the truth he wants you to believe.)

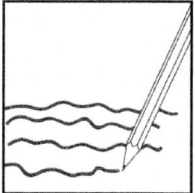

Write out the godly belief and read it aloud several times a day. Also search the Bible for verses reinforcing this new belief and personalize them. Write them out and read them aloud. Continue to do this until the truth saturates your being and shifts your behavior and experiences.

Word Curses

AWORD CURSE IS something negative said to you or about you that you believe and internalize so that it shapes your beliefs about yourself, your abilities, or your circumstances. Typically these also contribute to your failures in some way. You can also speak a word curse about yourself. Some common ones related to grief include:

- I'll never have enough.
- I can't have what's rightfully mine.
- I'm not as ____ as they are. Or I'm better than they are at _____.

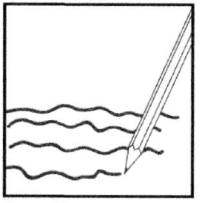

Spend time in prayer and allow the Holy Spirit to reveal any active curses that are impacting you. Once you identify any you have heard or said to yourself, you can break them off with the following prayer.

Father, I forgive _____ (this may be yourself), for cursing me by saying _____. (Repeat this for each of the people and curses you've written or what the Holy Spirit reveals to you as you pray.) I repent for believing this curse and for allowing it to shape my beliefs about myself, other people, my circumstances, and you. I ask for and receive your forgiveness. Thank you. I revoke and break all rights these curses had in my life and in my relationships and circumstances. I gather them up and cast them to the cross of Jesus along with any entities involved. I place the blood of Jesus between all that and me. I ask you, Jesus, to help me reverse and correct all the effects of these curses in my life, and help me appropriate the blessings you have for me in place of these curses. Thank you.

Soul Ties

SOUL TIES CAN be godly and healthy or ungodly. While sex is one way a soul tie forms, it is not the only way. We find godly soul ties in close, healthy relationships within healthy boundaries; those are beneficial, and we want to leave them alone or even strengthen them. Ungodly soul ties happen when two people make an inappropriate connection such as, a controlling or manipulative relationship that attempts to take away the free will of the other person. Not only does the ungodly soul tie give the other person more access to you than they should have, it also seems to give the enemy greater access to you.

I recommend praying to break any ungodly soul ties with anyone who comes to mind. If you have no soul ties with that person, then nothing happens, but you do have soul ties with them, then it's best to break them. You might have both godly and ungodly soul ties with the same person, especially your spouse or close family. Therefore, we specify we are breaking the ungodly soul ties.

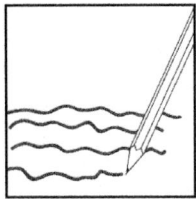

You can ask God for a list of people before you pray or just mention those that come to mind as you pray. You don't need to try to think of anyone and everyone. Just go with whoever immediately comes to mind and then move on. If God reminds you of others later, you can come back and pray again.

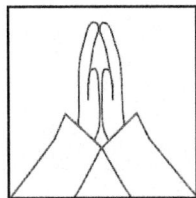

Father, I confess and repent of any ungodly soul ties I have with ____. I forgive ____ for their part in creating these soul ties. (Repeat for each person who comes to mind.) I take back what they have that is rightfully mine, and I send back to them what I have that is rightfully theirs, washed in the blood of Jesus and sent with a message of salvation, healing, and a blessing. I break off these soul ties. I seal up the connection point with the blood of Jesus. I revoke any rights the enemy has gained to me through these soul ties, and I gather up all entities involved and cast them to the cross of Jesus. I place the blood of Jesus between all that and me. In Jesus's name. Amen.

Emotional Wounds

ONE OF THE major access points the enemy has to each of us is through unhealed or ineffectively healed emotional wounds. We are hurt many times throughout our lives, but we can handle these hurts in a healthy or unhealthy manner. Sometimes these hurts shape our beliefs about ourselves and others inaccurately. Maybe the person disregarded our feelings, or no one knew how to help us work through what we thought, felt, or experienced. There's probably no end to the various ways people can hurt us. But do we allow God to help us work through those hurts, or do we stuff them, hoping they will go away?

Before we continue, I believe most people do the best they can with what they know: both we who hurt and the ones who are doing the hurting. Most people act in hurtful ways because of their own woundings. Most people are doing the best they know how given what they've been through. And this is one of the most important reasons for finding healing so that the pattern of hurting others ends with us. We get healed, and we learn how to treat others better, and the world becomes a better place.

In some cases, you might need someone else to help walk you through this process so that you don't become stuck and can keep moving. This depends on how healed you are, how fresh or how deep the wound is, current triggers related to the issue, etc. If you become stuck, this is a perfect time to phone a

friend, or seek a minister who can help you navigate this process. There is no shame in seeking help. The point is to get healed!

I recommend you take one memory or hurt at a time and go through the process. If more than one occasion of the same hurt comes to mind, you can often deal with them as a group. Just set your intention to include each incident that hurt occurred in your life. If you have different incidents, make a note of the others, and pick one to start with. You can keep going through your list until they are all done although you might need to take time for your system to recover after each of them. Again, this depends on how the hurts affected you.

The following is a basic template I use during sessions with clients. It is a guide, not a super rigid framework. This order is generally best because I've found it to be the most effective. But sometimes you need to go back to an earlier point and then move forward.

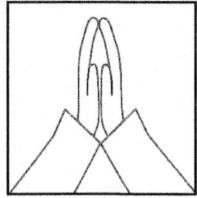

1. Ask Jesus or the Holy Spirit to take you to the first memory of hurt related to jealousy.
2. Tell Jesus how you are feeling in that memory.
3. Give all those negative emotions to Jesus. Some people find it helpful to picture pulling the negativity out of each cell or body part, starting at the toes and working upward, finally giving it all to Jesus or placing it at the foot of the cross. Sometimes you need to take each emotion, one at a time, and give it to Jesus. Other times, you can gather up the whole mess at once and give it to him. Keep doing this until you've given it all to him or placed it all at the cross.
4. Place the blood of Jesus between all the negativity and you. Ask Jesus to fill you with the opposite of what you've just released, e.g., his patience, love, hope, belonging, etc.

5. Invite Jesus into the memory to heal your hurt. Watch and wait to see what he does. He might want to take you to the Father.
6. You might need to revisit some earlier chapters and walk through forgiveness, ungodly lies and beliefs, etc.

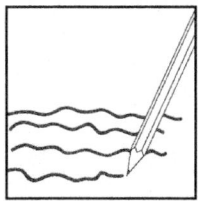

7. When you've finished all the healing, ask Jesus, Father, or the Holy Spirit to tell you what he thinks of you or of the situation as appropriate. Write what you see, hear, feel, or sense.

You can repeat this process for all hurts related to jealousy or any other issue you're dealing with. This is also effective for current hurts.

Demonic Oppression

I'VE OFTEN HEARD the demonic described as rats feeding on garbage. Part of what we've been doing so far in this book is getting rid of the garbage of the jealousy so that the rats have nothing left to attach to or feed on. Little by little, we've eliminated the contact points or rights we've given the enemy. Once we heal, break, and close off their rights, access, and contact points, we can easily kick them off.

We usually name the demonic by their function. Since we've been dealing with jealousy, we will get rid of the demons of jealousy and any under their authority or involved with them. Sometimes you can just toss the whole package, and sometimes you need to specifically name them one by one. Just repeat the prayer as often as you need to until you've eliminated them all. If you think of others later, just pray through the prayer again.

You'll notice this is not a complicated prayer. It's simple but powerful. Through Christ, you have authority over the enemy, especially when you've removed any rights the enemy has to be there. This is a legal proceeding not a power play, so volume is unnecessary. The enemy is not hearing-impaired, and he knows better than we do the authority we carry. So he often relies on hiddenness, darkness, and intimidation. But we've seen his plan and foiled his plots, so let's kick him out!

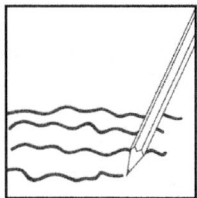

1. Father, forgive me for buying into the lies of jealousy and for giving jealousy access to my life through all the generational issues, soul ties, unforgiveness, ungodly beliefs, word curses, and woundings.

2. I forgive myself for buying into the lies of jealousy, and I accept your forgiveness.

3. I renounce, break, and cancel all agreements made with jealousy along with any other entity under its authority or affiliated with it. (Name any that come to mind, but don't linger here.)

4. I gather up jealousy and all entities involved in any way (including the list in #3 as needed) and cast them to the cross of Jesus. I place the blood of Jesus between all that and me.

5. I ask you, Jesus, to fill me with your peace and wholeness (and the opposite of the entities you've mentioned). Please teach me how to walk in your forgiveness and peace as I move forward in my life.

Anger at God

YOU MIGHT FIND you are holding on to anger, disappointment, or bitterness at God. Go back through these chapters and work through these feelings as they pertain to anxiety. Don't try to hide them; he knows about them already and longs to have that block or hindrance removed from between you. These feelings can be tricky to spot, so if you're stuck, reach out to a trusted friend or minister for some help.

Walking Out Your Healing

SHAMELESS PLUG: I took the following from my book *A Guide to Freedom.*[19] If you want more details and helpful ways to track your progress, check it out.

Give Yourself Grace

I want to strongly encourage you to give yourself grace and mercy in this journey. Don't try to get it all right. Don't do everything at once; just begin somewhere and keep going. If you trip and fall, repent and move on. One mistake is not a disaster. Even an entire series of mistakes need not be a disaster if you get up again and keep moving forward. Part of what you are overcoming in walking out your healing is relearning how to do life from a position of freedom and wholeness. You have deeply engrained habits to overcome. Often when we think we've lost our freedom, we've simply fallen back into old habits. Repent, get back up, and continue on. You'll learn new habits; it won't always be this hard.

---

19 Alice Briggs, A Guide to Freedom: 11 Steps to Greater Joy, Hope, and Peace (Lubbock: Alice Arlene, Ltd. Co. Press, 2016).

Saturate Your Atmosphere

Something tangible happens when we saturate our atmospheres with worship music. Worship resonates at a frequency that seems to transfer itself into the structure and atmosphere of the place. Worship lingers on long past when the last note died away. I've been to churches and cathedrals where they worshipped God for hundreds of years. Something unique and almost tangible permeates the atmosphere of many of them. This has nothing to do with a certain style or kind of music but is about the attitude, heart, and spirit of the artists singing and playing. That's why I've specified worship music here. Not all Christian music is worship although I enjoy most of it if I'm just listening to it. But if I want to shift the atmosphere, I pay more attention to music in which I most sense the Spirit.

Read the Word

The Bible is also the best place I know to learn about how God has worked with and through people since the beginning. We can learn much about who God is and what he is like by reading his Word. This is especially true if you read several translations and paraphrases. I'm not saying you have to sit down and study the Bible for hours a day. That goal is not realistic for most of us. You can sign up for a verse of the day to go to your email from various websites. I receive emails with a chapter a day from www.bibleplan.org. They have quite a few different plans to choose from. I enjoy the convenience of receiving these in my inbox each morning, especially when traveling.

Personalize Scripture

As I'm reading the Bible, sometimes a verse jumps out at me and seems to apply to what I'm going through. The verse might be something I desire to see manifest in my life. I not only highlight these verses but also personalize them. This helps me absorb their truths much more effectively.

I take 3 × 5 cards and write out the verse or verses so that they pertain directly to me, putting my name in them as much as possible. I read them aloud as often as needed. In some of my darkest times, I've had so many verses that I bought a photo album to put them in so that I could easily flip through them.

For example, Psalm 100:4 reads, "Enter his gates with thanksgiving; go into his courts with praise; give thanks to him and praise his name."

I can personalize this in at least two ways.

First, I can say: I will enter his gates with thanksgiving. I will go into his courts with praise. I will give thanks to him, and I will praise his name.

Or: Alice will enter his gates with thanksgiving. Alice will go into his courts with praise. Alice will give thanks to him, and Alice will praise his name.

I find that using the second way is more effective.

Two-Way Journaling

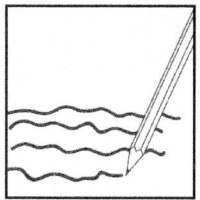

Listening to the Spirit is an excellent way to gain more freedom. Two-way journaling is a great way to refine your listening. I learned this technique by watching Dr. Mark Virkler's DVDs, *4 Keys to Hearing God's Voice.*[20] He basically encourages you to make sure your heart is right and ask God a question. "What do you think of me?" or "How do you see me?" or something along those lines is a great way to start. Quiet yourself and listen to him. Write whatever you hear. Don't analyze it, just write. You can proofread later if you want to.

Spiritual things register on the right side of your brain. Analyzation and proofreading are more left-brain activities. For those of us who spend a lot of time using the left side of the brain, switching to the right side takes practice, so stay over there, and use the right side as long as possible when you get there! If this is new to you, Dr. Virkler recommends that you share your journaling

---

20 Mark Virkler, "4 Keys to Hearing God—You Can Hear God's Voice!" Communion with God Ministries, accessed January 11, 2019, https://www.cwgministries.org/Four-Keys-to-Hearing-Gods-Voice.

with a few trusted advisors who know you and love you and who can hear from God for themselves. Seek counsel from them if you are making a major decision of any kind. This is wise advice. In the beginning, you want them to tell you if they think what you've heard is the voice of the Spirit.

Take Thoughts Captive

We normally have three sources of thoughts in our heads. They can all sound like us, so we need to learn to discern the source of each. Once we understand whose voice we're hearing, we need to learn what it means to take a thought captive. It means that we do not let that thought linger in our minds. Once we recognize a thought as coming from the enemy, I find it helpful to just say "No! Nope! Nada!" out loud, if need be. I might follow that with a statement, such as "I bind up that thought and cast it to the cross. That thought is not mine or God's, and I will not receive it." I then focus on the opposite thought. If I can use one of my personalized scriptures, this adds strength and power to help me focus on the truth and create positive thoughts.

Forgive Quickly and Often

Keep on forgiving. As I mentioned earlier in this book, this is a process, so we might need to remind ourselves that we've chosen to forgive. We might also need to forgive those who hurt us as we move forward.

Exercise Your Spiritual Gifts

Seek to discover and use the gifts that God has given you, whatever they might be. In this way, you step into your destiny and do the good things he planned for you to do.

Practice Thankfulness

Gratitude is a powerful force. Use it. Make a list of what you have to be thankful for and add to it often. See if you can find something new to be thankful for every day.

Share your Testimony

Tell the world about the good things God has done for you in overcoming anxiety. Not only does this help you focus on the victories you've achieved, but you give others courage to seek their own healing.

Resist the Enemy

He's had you under his control through anxiety for a while. No matter how long he's had you in his clutches, he will want you back. That doesn't mean you weren't healed and set free; it's just what he does. As I previously said, his job description is to kill, steal, and destroy, and your healing and freedom is at the top of that list! When you spot his attacks, recognize them for the lies they are, pick up your armor, and stand in the truth and fight!

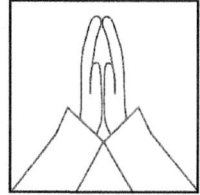

Father, I ask you to set your seal upon the work I have done and will continue to do as I walk out my healing. I believe you are faithful to continue this work and bring me to greater and greater realms of healing and wholeness. I cancel all curses, devices, or assignments of the enemy and break off any retaliation in the name of Jesus. I seal all doors and windows in the spirit with Jesus's blood and thank you and praise you for your protection. Please minister to me as my system adjusts to this new level of healing and wholeness and comes into alignment with your design. In Jesus's name. Amen.

Emotional Roots Series

Find these and others as they are released here: https://emotionalandspiritu-
alhealing.com/emotional-roots-physical-symptoms/

The Emotional Roots of Viruses

The Emotional Roots of Breast Cancer

The Emotional Roots of Fibromyalgia

The Emotional Roots of Sinusitis

The Emotional Roots of Cysts

The Emotional Roots of Lupus

Emotional and Spiritual Healing Book Series

Find all these and others here: https://emotionalandspiritualhealing.com/book/
Overcoming Perfectionism
Overcoming Rejection
Overcoming Shame
Overcoming Anxiety
Overcoming Insecurity
Overcoming Anger
Overcoming Hopelessness
Overcoming Control
Overcoming Triggers
Overcoming Guilt
Overcoming Confusion
Overcoming Grief
Overcoming Jealousy
Overcoming Pride

About the Author

Alice Briggs is a business owner, publisher, writer, teacher, and artist. She loves to assist others to achieve their goals, which is the common thread in all she does.

She has an emotional and spiritual healing business helping people address the emotional and spiritual roots of behaviors and physical conditions. Most of her 30+ published titles are in this Christian inner healing/self-help space. She also partners with a mastermind partner of many years in a business class, helping people deal with their "head trash" or blocks so they can succeed in whatever they're doing.

She is also a fine artist and has worked in mixed media as a painter professionally for more than 25 years. She loves creating artworks that bring peace into a space. She's published 5 art books to date and has illustrated 5 children's books.

Through Kingdom Covers, she uses her graphic design and artistic skill set to design covers and interiors for fellow indie authors, and loves to help new authors take their books from manuscript to published. She has coached many new authors across the publishing line, and hopes to see many more succeed in this arena in the future.

She is co-founder and Creative Director of *Indie Author Magazine*, and is involved with Indie Author Tools and the new Author Tech Summit. She recently added two more publications under her publisher's umbrella: *Lubbock's Home and Family Magazine*, and *Weddings by Wendy Rose*.

You can see all of her books where ever books are sold

Other Books By Alice Briggs

Emotional and Spiritual Healing
A Guide to Freedom
Accessing Your Spiritual Inheritance
Identity

Artwork - see AliceArlene.com or ArtfulPrayers.com
Embracing the Colors of Peace
Co-Creation: Partnering with God
Peace in the Storm
Artful Prayers
Artful Prayers for 50 States

Helpful guides
Celebrate Every Win Planner
Indie Route 101
Supernatural Business

Children's books with Lisa Simmons
Sadie Sees Paris
Bo Goes to Hawaii

Children's books with Larry Briggs and Jennie Briggs
The Monkey with the Long, Long Tail
The Monkey with the Long, Long Tail Goes to the Park
The Monkey with the Long, Long Tail is a Hero

Printed in Great Britain
by Amazon

20995233R00122